Men of Honor

MEN'S GROUP STUDY

MEN OF HONOR

MIKE CLEVELAND

Men of Honor
By Mike Cleveland

Inquire at: Focus Publishing
                Rights and Permissions
                PO Box 665
                Bemidji, MN 56619

ISBN: 1-885904-61-4

Cover Design by Barb Van Thomma

In a large house there are articles not only of gold and silver, but also of wood and clay; some are for noble purposes and some for ignoble. If a man cleanses himself from the latter, he will be an instrument for noble purposes, made holy, useful to the Master and prepared to do any good work.

2 Timothy 2:20-21

Table of Contents

Men of Honor
Men's Group Study

Mike Cleveland
Founder and President of Setting Captives Free

Introduction

Becoming a Man of Honor is a worthy, but lofty goal. It is a worthy goal because being a **Man of Honor**, according to 2 Timothy 2:20-21, makes one **"an instrument for noble purposes," "made holy," "useful to the Master,"** and **"prepared to do any good work."** It is a lofty goal because it requires men to "cleanse themselves," thereby going against all the forces of evil, the allurements of our culture, and even our own wrong thoughts and desires.

The four studies in this series are designed to help men attain the worthy and lofty goal of becoming a **Man of Honor**. These studies were first presented in January, 2006, to approximately two hundred men at Parkside Church in Chagrin Falls, Ohio. These men faithfully came to the classes every Monday night for four weeks, and God used His Word in these studies to change many of their lives. It is our hope and prayer that He will continue to do so, as more men study this material and implement the biblical truths contained within.

As you, your church, or your small group go through these studies, please consider writing us at webservant@settingcaptivesfree.com to provide feedback with regard to the course, how it was received, and with any suggestions for improvement.

Thank you.

Sincerely,

Mike Cleveland

Men of Honor
Overview and General Instruction

The studies in the **Men of Honor** course are focused and intentional. The purpose is to help men to become **Men of Honor** by "cleansing themselves" (2 Timothy 2:21) from all impurity. The Bible is the textbook, the heart is the target, and the Holy Spirit is the Teacher.

The studies are to help men to find freedom from any impurity, thereby becoming **Men of Honor**. It is important to understand that there are many different habitual sins from which we are required to be cleansed. Men struggle with pornography and sexual impurity of all kinds, with overeating and overdrinking, with drug abuse, gambling, smoking, and all manner of other habitual sins. There are also heart sins which need to be addressed. Issues such as sinful anger, bitterness, deceit, covetousness, etc., are sins which are not always easily seen, but may destroy Christian life and inhibit fruitfulness. Through the **Men of Honor** course, these sins should all be addressed, and the men should be invited to turn from them, and to turn to Christ.

It is recommended that anyone who would like to teach or facilitate this course go through the free 25-lesson mentorship course at www.settingcaptivesfree.com. This course teaches the basics of biblical mentoring and discipling of others, giving valuable preparation to those who would lead in both the main group setting, and also in the small groups. In order to gain access to this course, simply call 330.620.8448 or email webservant@settingcaptivesfree.com .

During the small group discussions, the facilitator/leader is encouraged to keep the discussions on topic and free from any potential ramblings of anyone in the group. The objective is to ask the question, have the men look in the Bible for the answer, and then ask for thoughts on the Scriptures. If not careful, the conversation may quickly turn from what God's Word teaches to an individual's particular viewpoint instead. The aim of the study is to look into the Scriptures and see what God says, and then discuss in the group how to apply the truths learned.

At the end of the course, it is recommended that you pass out the "Response Card" which we have included at the back of this manual. At Parkside Church, we asked the men to fill out the card and, if they were struggling with a particular sin issue, to indicate it on the response card. We informed them that, if they indicated they were struggling with any particular sin, someone would contact them and invite them to go through one of the courses at Setting Captives Free - www.settingcaptivesfree.com.

The Men of Honor studies are designed to be used in group study, with interaction among the men. They are split into four complete studies, which may be accomplished on one night a week for four weeks, or alternatively, the whole series may be completed in a single day.

A sample format is listed below:

- 7:00 PM – 7:30 PM: Small group leaders meeting and prayer. Meet to discuss the material, answer any questions, and pray for the men who will be attending.
- 7:30 PM – 8:10 PM: Main Group Teaching Session
- 8:10 PM – 8:40 PM: Small Group Discussion Session
- 8:40PM – 8:45PM: Main Group Wrap-Up, Introduction of the Next Week's Material.

Each lesson is broken down into the following four components:

1. Main Session Notes. These notes are for the leader who will teach the material to the entire group during the main teaching session. They are designed for anyone to teach and may simply be read aloud, if the teacher so desires.

2. Fill-In-the-Blank Notes. These notes correspond to the main session notes.

3. Discussion Leader Notes. These notes are for the discussion leader/facilitator, and are intended to be studied prior to the meetings, in preparation for leading the small groups.

4. Question Sheet. These questions will frame the small group discussions.

Men of Honor—Session One
An Invitation to the Thirsty

In the movie "Four Feathers," Harry Faversham (Heath Ledger) is the son of a British war hero. Along with his friends, he is among the top officers being shipped to the Sudan where rebellion has broken out. Harry, unlike his friends, doesn't want to be a soldier as he is afraid, so he resigns his post. Shocked and amazed, three of his friends give Harry three white feathers (a symbol that Harry has "ducked" his duties), and then, in a move that wounds him to the core of his heart, his fiancée gives him a fourth feather. Shamed, humiliated, stripped of honor, Harry feels lost and hopeless. Soon thereafter, however, Harry has a "lifetime moment" where he decides that his honor is more important than his life. He sets out for the Sudan where he covertly assists his friends in battle, even saving the lives of several of them. At the end of the movie, Harry is recognized as the one who saved their lives, and honor and respect are restored to him. He returns his feathers and, in the case of war heroes, it is customary to give them a medal of honor.

We all want to be honorable men, don't we? Some of us know what it's like to be a Man of Honor. Many of us were honorable at one time. But now, if we are honest, it is possible that the word "honorable' does not describe our lives. Maybe we have made poor choices, compromised our integrity, and we desperately wish to be restored. In this study, we will learn how we can be restored and become a man of honor. You can walk with your head high before your wife, your children, and your work associates because God will remove your shame and restore you (Leviticus 26:13.) Yes, it is truly possible to turn our feathers in for medals because in God's army, those who have acted wrongly may be fully restored.

For this study, we will discuss the topic "**Men of Honor**." Let us turn to 2 Timothy 2 and read verses 20-21, as these particular verses will be our "theme passage" for this four-session study.

> [20] In a large house there are articles not only of gold and silver, but also of wood and clay; some are for noble purposes and some for ignoble. [21] If a man cleanses himself from the latter, he will be an instrument for noble purposes, made holy, useful to the Master and prepared to do any good work (2 Timothy 2:20-21).

As the men of the <u>church</u> go, so goes the church. Men are called to <u>lead</u>. We're to lead our homes and families; we are to lead in business and community; we are to lead in the church. But did you notice from 2 Timothy 2:20-21 the main requirement for good leadership, for being **Men of Honor**? It is purity! The passage states, "If a man cleanses himself...he will be an instrument of noble (or honorable) purposes." We are excited to study this topic together, to learn how purity enables us to become **Men of Honor**.

Let's look just now at a preview of the four sessions:

Session 1:   **An Invitation to the Thirsty**
Session 2:   **Foundations of Freedom**
Session 3:   **Repentance Versus Remorse**
Session 4:   **Walking in the Light**

The objectives of the four sessions are:

1. To see unbelieving men become <u>pure</u> followers of Jesus Christ
2. To see every <u>believing</u> man enjoy ongoing purity
3. To see every man <u>equipped</u> to help other men find freedom from impurity

Or, in other words... that We Might Be **Men of <u>Honor</u>**.

What is honor? What is purity? It is maintaining a right, upright, honorable relationship with God and others. It is enjoying the presence of God and the absence of habitual sin.

Why is this study being offered? Why should we desire to be Men of Honor? In other words, why is purity so important? By way of introduction, let us examine four reasons why it is important to "cleanse ourselves" so that we might be **Men of Honor**:

1. Purity Precedes <u>Power</u>:

> [18] Many of those who believed now came and openly confessed their evil deeds. [19] A number who had practiced sorcery brought their scrolls together and burned them publicly. When they calculated the value of the scrolls, the total came to fifty thousand drachmas. [20] In this way the word of the Lord spread widely and grew in power (Acts 19:18-20).

We notice from this passage that, as a result of Paul's preaching, many people became believers in Jesus Christ. In this particular instance, we see many people confessing their sins and burning the scrolls which they had used to practice sorcery. They wanted to rid their lives of all that God hates, so they purified their homes of all materials dealing with sorcery, desiring to be rid of it entirely, no matter the cost. But, what is important for our study is to notice the last verse in this passage. After the people had confessed their sin and removed their impurity, the Bible says "in this way the word of the Lord spread widely and grew in **power**."

It is true in the life of any man, that when he <u>cleanses</u> himself, the <u>power</u> of God is present. Purity precedes power. Purity brings with it an uninterrupted flow of the presence and power of God. It is possible to be men of power. We are not necessarily talking about men who are successful in business, who drive luxury cars, and have memberships in country clubs (though it is not our intention to put them down). Instead, we are talking about men who are not continually knocked down by the forces of evil, men who live in obedience to God and in victory over habitual sin. Purity is God's design for our lives, and He enables us to daily turn from sin and to walk in obedience to Christ. We are talking about the men John describes in 1 John 2:14:

> I write to you, young men, because you are strong, and the word of God lives in you, and you have overcome the evil one.

Another example of the "Purity Precedes Power" principle is the following story of Jacob:

> [1] Then God said to Jacob, "Go up to Bethel and settle there, and build an altar there to God, who appeared to you when you were fleeing from your brother Esau." [2] So Jacob said to his household and to all who were with him, "Get rid of the foreign gods you have with you, and purify yourselves and change your   clothes. [3] Then come, let us go up to Bethel, where I will build an altar to God, who answered me in the day of my distress and who has been with me wherever I have gone." [4] So they gave Jacob all the foreign gods they had and the rings in their ears, and Jacob buried them under the oak at Shechem. [5] Then they set out, and the terror of God fell upon the towns all around them so that no one pursued them (Genesis 35:1-5, NIV).

In this passage, Jacob leads his family in righteousness. He tells all who were with him to purify themselves, to get rid of their foreign gods, and to change their attire. Then he leads them to Bethel, the place of worship. The amazing thing about this story is the effect this shepherd-man and his family have on the surrounding towns. The Bible says, immediately following the record of the family cleansing themselves, "The terror of God fell upon the towns all around them…"

Men of God, who will take seriously the admonition to "cleanse themselves," will experience the presence and power of God in a noticeable way.

2. Purity Precedes <u>Perception</u>: In Matthew 5:8 Jesus says, "Blessed are the **pure** in heart, for they will *see* God." It is possible to be men of keen discernment, men who see God in their daily lives, men who see God's plans and purposes in all things. Sin clouds our vision. We will never see God rightly when we are living in willful disobedience.

3. Purity Precedes (godly) <u>Passion</u>. Let's examine 1 Peter 1:22:

> Now that you have purified yourselves by obeying the truth so that you have sincere love for your brothers, love one another deeply, from the heart.

It is when we purposefully set out to remove impurity from our hearts and lives that we are able to effectively love others fervently. Men who rid their lives of pornography, adultery, self-gratification, drunkenness, drugs, overeating, etc. are able to be conduits for the love of God, which fills their hearts and is able to flow, unrestricted, out to others.

4. Purity Precedes <u>Profitability</u>. We get the term, "profitability" from the King James Version of 2 Timothy 2:20-21, where it states that those who "cleanse themselves" will be "meet" or **profitable** for the Master's use.

To summarize, the reason we are discussing the subject of becoming **Men of Honor** for the next four sessions is so that we, as men, might have spiritual **power** in our lives, that we might have spiritual **perception**, that we might have godly **passion** for one another, and that we would be **profitable** to the Master.

As we begin our main study, let us pause and each one of us pray and ask God for His help to see how important purity is, to show us areas in our lives where we have been disobedient, and to turn our hearts toward Him in prayer.

Let's look at John 4:4-30, and notice three specific points.

> [4]Now he (Jesus) had to go through Samaria. [5]So he came to a town in Samaria called Sychar, near the plot of ground Jacob had given to his son Joseph. [6]Jacob's well was there, and Jesus, tired as he was from the journey, sat down by the well. It was about the sixth hour. [7]When a Samaritan woman came to draw water, Jesus said to her, "Will you give me a drink?" [8](His disciples had gone into the town to buy food.)
>
> [9]The Samaritan woman said to him, "You are a Jew and I am a Samaritan woman. How can you ask me for a drink?" (For Jews do not associate with Samaritans.) [10]Jesus answered her, "If you knew the gift of God, and who it is that asks you for a drink, you would have asked him and he would have given you living water."
>
> [11]"Sir," the woman said, "you have nothing to draw with and the well is deep. Where can you get this living water? [12]Are you greater than our

8

father Jacob, who gave us the well and drank from it himself, as did also his sons and his flocks and herds?"

[13]Jesus answered, "Everyone who drinks this water will be thirsty again, [14]but whoever drinks the water I give him will never thirst. Indeed, the water I give him will become in him a spring of water, welling up to eternal life." [15]The woman said to him, "Sir, give me this water so that I won't get thirsty and have to keep coming here to draw water." [16] He told her, "Go, call your husband and come back."

[17]"I have no husband," she replied. Jesus said to her, "You are right when you say you have no husband. [18]The fact is, you have had five husbands, and the man you now have is not your husband. What you have just said is quite true." [19]"Sir," the woman said, "I can see that you are a prophet. [20]Our fathers worshiped on this mountain, but you Jews claim that the place where we must worship is in Jerusalem."

[21]Jesus declared, "Believe me, woman, a time is coming when you will worship the Father neither on this mountain nor in Jerusalem [22]You Samaritans worship what you do not know; we worship what we do know, for salvation is from the Jews. [23]Yet a time is coming and has now come, when the true worshipers will worship the Father in spirit and truth, for they are the kind of worshipers the Father seeks. [24]God is spirit, and his worshipers must worship in spirit and I truth."

[25]The woman said, "I know that Messiah (called Christ) is coming. When he comes, he will explain everything to us." [26]Then Jesus declared, "I who speak to you am he."

[27]Just then the disciples returned, and were surprised to find him talking with a woman. But no one asked, "What do you want?" or "Why are you talking with her?"

[28]Then, leaving her water jar, the woman went back to the town and said to the people, [29]"Come, see a man who told me everything I ever did. Could this be the Christ?" [30]They came out of the town and made their way toward him.

Here we have presented in the text:

1. An Apparent <u>Sinner</u>. This woman at the well is an apparent sinner because:

She was living <u>immorally</u> (verse 18).

She was reasoning carnally (verses 11, 12, 20). Jesus talks about "living water;" she thinks about physical water. Jesus speaks about spiritual worship; she talks about mountains on which to worship. She thinks in earthly, carnal, and unspiritual terms. Sin draws our heads downward, causing us to miss the reality of spiritual things, blinding our eyes to the beauty of Jesus Christ and to the glory of His gospel.

She was diverting religiously (verses 18-20. Jesus brings up her past life; she diverts the subject to a question of which mountain is the correct one for worship.

She was thirsting spiritually. The important concept to understand from this passage is that verses 13 and 18 are related. In verse 13, Jesus is not merely making a statement about the physical water in the well, saying that if anyone drinks of it he will thirst again. That would be an overly obvious and unnecessary statement. Instead, Jesus is connecting physical thirst with spiritual thirst, which can be seen by comparing verses 13 and 18. This woman is going from one man to another, always hoping the next man will "satisfy her thirst," but each time she is "thirsty again." It is much like the man who goes from one porn image to another, or one bar and bottle to another, or one casino to another. His satisfaction is only temporary, and soon he is "thirsting again." Pornography, drinking and drugs, etc. are like salt-water which only causes more thirst, so that he must keep coming back for more.

2. An Amazing **Savior**. Jesus is shown here to be an amazing Savior because:

He seeks the lost. Jesus said he had to go through Samaria; He went to where she was. He initiated the discussion about thirsting, He brought up her issues with men, and He offered her living water. Romans 10:20 quotes Isaiah, "I was found by those who did not seek me; I revealed myself to those who did not ask for me." A popular song has the following message: "You did not wait for me, to draw near to You, but You clothed Yourself in frail humanity." You did not wait for me to call out to You, but You let me hear Your voice calling me." Christianity is the only religion where the Leader seeks out the sinful, the disobedient, and the rebellious, and offers them forgiveness, peace with God, and eternal life.

He quenches thirst, (satisfies her heart, fulfills her longings, etc.) Jesus promised, "Whoever drinks the water I give him, will never thirst." He is able to meet the needs and fulfill the desires of the human heart. Psalm 107:9 says, "He satisfies the thirsty, and fills the hungry with good things." He is an amazing Savior!

He turns from sin. The way Jesus turns us from sin is much like He did with the woman at the well. He offers us something much better. He quenches spiritual thirst so that we can leave our old life of sin behind, much like the woman at the well, who began drinking of Jesus and left her old water pot behind.

He makes her useful. This woman, who had previously been so ashamed that she went to the well when the rest of the town was not there, was now proclaiming Jesus Christ to all of them. Her message was, "Come see a Man…" Oh, how true it is that when a man begins drinking living water he not only has enough for himself, but plenty to share with others, as well. This woman is now being useful, her words carry influence, she makes an impact on her neighbors in the town.

3. An Absolute <u>Salvation</u>. She experienced an absolute salvation, which is evidenced by these facts:

She <u>left</u> her water pot behind. We don't want to make too much of this, as it is entirely possible that she was simply in a hurry to tell others of Jesus the Messiah, and she surely did need to continue drinking physical water again. But what we can say is that when anyone begins truly drinking the living water, they will inevitably leave something behind.

She confessed her <u>sin</u> to others. Her statement was "Come, see a Man who told me everything I ever did." She was now admitting that she had done certain things, and that Jesus knew them, indeed He knew *her*. There was no blame-shifting here, no denial of her past, no changing of the subject. Now she openly confessed that she had done certain things, and that Jesus had revealed them to her. One of the things that we notice quite often at Setting Captives Free is that, when a man begins to enjoy freedom from impurity, he stops all blame-shifting and accusing of others, and instead acknowledges his own sin and accepts responsibility for it.

She testified of <u>Christ</u>. Her message was "Come see a Man..." She was thrilled with Jesus. He had revealed her past. He had given her hope of being free of the continual "thirst" of always looking for another man. He had taught her that true "drinking" of the living water ends in spiritual worship of God (like the "Ahhh" that comes after a refreshing drink). And now she was telling the whole town about Him. She said, "Come, see a Man..." which is equivalent to saying, "Come, have a drink." Her message was an invitation to the thirsty.

She brought <u>others</u> to Christ. The whole town listened to her and went out to see Jesus. Possibly they could tell this woman was different, and no doubt they were intrigued with her message and wanted to see and hear for themselves. Wow, what a change has come into the life of this woman. This is "absolute salvation."

Jesus restored her honor! She admitted and confessed her sin. She found forgiveness in Christ. She received a message, a purpose, and a reason to hold her head up high. This was not because of anything that she had done, but was all through God's grace to her.

Let us conclude now by noting several truths for application:

Truth #1:

Sin *is* and also *causes* spiritual <u>thirst</u> (unsatisfied cravings, unfulfilled longings, deep unmet yearnings of the heart). Sin is exciting and pleasurable for a time, but does not contain within it that which is thirst-quenching truth.

Truth #2:

Turning to <u>impurity</u> of any kind, like drinking salt-water, only causes more <u>thirst</u>. "Anyone who drinks **'this water'** will thirst again." (Jeremiah 2:13). Many men have longings within them; longings to be valued and appreciated, longings for intimacy, or desires for genuine love. But turning to pornography, or alcohol or gambling, etc., will never meet these deep needs, and will leave the "aftertaste" of guilt and shame in our systems. We must recognize that the desire to escape into the fantasy world of porn, to drown our troubles in alcohol, or to run off into the "other world" of gambling is simply the evidence of spiritual thirst. We must understand that spiritual thirst is not quenched through impurity, but rather through receiving what Jesus Christ provides to those who come to Him.

It is also important to note that there may be disastrous consequences to this life of "thirsting." As impurity always causes more thirst, many people do things that have catastrophic results in their lives. In their pursuit of that which will quench their thirst, many have turned their backs on God, have thumbed their noses at His grace, and have pursued their lusts with reckless abandon. Many have hurt their families, ruined their ministries, or lost their jobs while they go from one sin to another. As we continue in our study on Men of Honor, we will notice many other consequences to sin, which should be good reminders regarding our need to quench our spiritual thirst only in Jesus Christ.

Truth #3:

Jesus Christ is and also provides <u>Living</u> <u>Water</u>: "Whoever drinks **'the water I give'** him, will never thirst." Do we want to know how to stop gambling? Do we want to know how to stop overdrinking, overeating, how to stop viewing pornography, how to be free from homosexuality, or how to overcome workaholism? "Whoever drinks the water I give him, will never thirst." We will stop thirsting when we learn to quench our thirst in Jesus. We will cease longing, yearning, and craving when we learn to drink. Our thirst will be quenched. Our souls will be satisfied.

> You prepare a table before me in the presence of my enemies. You anoint my head with oil; my cup overflows (Psalm 23:5).

> Who satisfies your desires with good things so that your youth is renewed like the eagle's (Psalm 103:5).

> [37] On the last and greatest day of the Feast, Jesus stood and said in a loud voice, "If anyone is thirsty, let him come to me and drink. [38] Whoever believes in me, as the Scripture has said, streams of living water will flow from within him." [39] By this he meant the Spirit, whom those who believed in him were later to receive. Up to that time the Spirit had not been given, since Jesus had not yet been glorified (John 7:37-39).

A Closing Thought:

It is entirely possible, indeed *inevitable*, to be free from impurity (John 8:36), if we learn to drink from Jesus Christ. This freedom will not be found in "anonymous" groups, steps, vows, decisions, or promises to do better, etc. It will be found the same way the woman at the well found it: through an encounter with Jesus Christ, through genuine repentance of sin, through learning how to drink the Living Water (that is, how to satisfy ourselves in Christ). A **Man of Honor** is one who refuses sinful and impure "water sources" and who instead drinks of the pure, life-giving water of the Lord Jesus Christ.

Illustration: Bill was a professional lawyer, an elder in his church, who had a wonderful wife and four small children. But Bill was ensnared in pornography, and had been for four years. One day through discussions with a Christian friend, he broke down and told this friend of his problem with pornography. His friend assured him he would pray for him, and asked him out to lunch the following week. Over the course of their lunch meeting, this friend presented the three "foundational principles" of being free from any habitual sin, the same principles we are going to study in session two. Bill committed to applying the principles, with his friend as his accountability partner. As a result, Bill now has a newfound love for his wife, is raising his children in a godly manner, and, despite ongoing struggles with the flesh, he has been entirely free from pornography for nearly two years. God is enabling Bill to "cleanse himself" from all impurity, and, as such, is becoming a **"Man of Honor."**

Bill wrote, "When I was ensnared in pornography, I never thought I could get free of it. I thought it was a "guy thing" that would just always be with me. And even though I was a Christian, I thought this area would just be my "thorn in the flesh." I just never knew I could experience the presence of God so intimately, and the love of my wife so passionately, as I do now. I struggle daily with temptation in many areas, I suppose we all do, but Jesus Christ has made me "free indeed." I love Him very much, and I love my wife and children very much, too. And I am noticing the power of God attends my preaching and other ministry activities, too. What a joy to be free!"

Men of Honor – Session One Worksheet

[20] In a large house there are articles not only of gold and silver, but also of wood and clay; some are for noble purposes and some for ignoble. [21] If a man cleanses himself from the latter, he will be an instrument for noble purposes, made holy, useful to the Master and prepared to do any good work (2 Timothy 2:20-21).

As the men of the _____ go, so goes the church. Men are called to _____.

The objectives of the four sessions are:

4. To see unbelieving men become _____ followers of Jesus Christ
5. To see every _____ man enjoy ongoing purity
6. To see every man _____ to help other men find freedom from impurity.

Or, in other words…**"That We Might Be Men of _____"**

Purity Precedes _____.

[18] Many of those who believed now came and openly confessed their evil deeds. [19] A number who had practiced sorcery brought their scrolls together and burned them publicly. When they calculated the value of the scrolls, the total came to fifty thousand drachmas. [20] In this way the word of the Lord spread widely and grew in power (Acts 19:18-20).

It is true in the life of any man that, when he _____ himself, the _____ of God is present.

I write to you, young men, because you are strong, and the word of God lives in you, and you have overcome the evil one (1 John 2:14).

[1] Then God said to Jacob, "Go up to Bethel and settle there, and build an altar there to God, who appeared to you when you were fleeing from your brother Esau." [2] So Jacob said to his household and to all who were with him, "Get rid of the foreign gods you have with you, and purify yourselves and change your clothes. [3] Then come, let us go up to Bethel, where I will build an altar to God, who answered me in the day of my distress and who has been with me wherever I have gone." [4] So they gave Jacob all the foreign gods they had and the rings in their ears, and Jacob buried them under the oak at Shechem. [5] Then they set out, and the terror of God fell upon the towns all around them so that no one pursued them (Genesis 35:1-5).

Purity Precedes _____.

Purity Precedes (godly) _____.

Now that you have purified yourselves by obeying the truth so that you have sincere love for your brothers, love one another deeply, from the heart (1 Peter 1:22).

It is when we purposefully set out to remove _____ from our hearts and lives that we are able to effectively _____ others fervently.

Purity Precedes _____.

Here we have presented in the text:

1. An Apparent _____.

    She was living _____

    She was _____ carnally

    She was diverting _____

    She was _____ spiritually

2. An Amazing _____.

    He seeks the _____

    He _____ thirst

    He turns from _____

    He makes her _____

3. An Absolute _____.

    She _____ her water pot behind

    She confessed her _____ to others

    She testified of _____

She brought_____ _____ to Christ

Truth #1:

Sin is and also causes spiritual _____

Truth #2:

Turning to _____ of any kind, like drinking salt-

water, only causes more _____.

Truth #3:

Jesus Christ is and also provides _____.

Who satisfies your desires with good things so that your youth is renewed like the eagle's (Psalm 103:5).

> [37] On the last and greatest day of the Feast, Jesus stood and said in a loud voice, "If anyone is thirsty, let him come to me and drink. [38] Whoever believes in me, as the Scripture has said, streams of living water will flow from within him." [39] By this he meant the Spirit, whom those who believed in him were later to receive. Up to that time the Spirit had not been given, since Jesus had not yet been glorified (John 7:37-39).

A **Man of Honor** is one who refuses sinful and impure _____
and who instead drinks of the pure, _____-_____ water of the Lord
Jesus Christ _____

Men of Honor - Session One
Discussion Questions

(Main Session - 2 Timothy 2:20-21, Acts 19:18-20, 1 John 2:14, Genesis 35:1-5, 1 Peter 1:22, Psalms 23:5, Psalms 103:5, John 7:37-39; Small Groups - Isaiah 55:1-3, Ephesians 4:19, Jeremiah 2:13.)

Question 1. According to Isaiah 55:1-3, who is issued the invitation? Is this "thirsty" condition physical or spiritual?

Question 2. The invitation in Isaiah 55:1-3 is for those who "thirst" to "come to the waters." But where are the "waters?" How does verse 3 help us to understand the answer?

Question 3. If we "drink" by "listening to God" in His Word, what are the results of drinking in the Word, according to verse 2?

Question 4. What are the results of drinking in the Word, according to verse 3?

Question 5. How does this verse go with today's teaching? "Having lost all sensitivity, they have given themselves over to sensuality so as to indulge in every kind of impurity, *with a continual lust for more*" Ephesians 4:19 (emphasis added).

Question 6. What are your thoughts about this quote from Charles Spurgeon? "Men are in a restless pursuit after satisfaction in earthly things. They will exhaust themselves in the deceitful delights of sin, and, finding them to be vanity, and emptiness, they will become very perplexed and disappointed. But they will continue their fruitless search. Though wearied, they still stagger forward under the influence of spiritual madness, and though there is no result to be reached except that of everlasting disappointment, yet they press forward. They have no forethought for their eternal state; the present hour absorbs them. They turn to another and another of earth's broken cisterns, hoping to find water where not a drop was ever discovered yet."

Question 7. Verse 2 of Isaiah 55 above asks an important question: "Why spend money on what does not satisfy? Have you spent money (or time) on that which does not satisfy?

Notes:

Men of Honor — Session Two
Foundations of Freedom

Welcome to the second session in our series of four, entitled "**Men of Honor**." Please open your Bibles to Matthew, chapter 15. In this session, we are going to discuss how to be a **Man of Honor**. There are three foundational principles to finding freedom from impurity, to walking free from sin's domination.

Before we discuss the three foundational principles to freedom from ongoing and habitual sin, let us take note of some of the teachings available today from various sources, which attempt to help with areas of habitual sin.

While in bondage to pornography and self-gratification for 15 years, I tried many of the methods we will examine here. Yet my involvement in impurity continued, as the false cures presented to me only served to make me *knowledgeably* enslaved.

False Solutions the world offers today:

1. <u>Rubber</u> <u>Band</u> Method

This method tells us to place a rubber band around our wrists and, whenever we are tempted, to snap the rubber band. This helps us begin to associate temptation with pain in order to learn to avoid areas of temptation. I remember snapping my wrist continually, sometimes at 2:00 a.m., as powerful temptations would assault me, but pain is no deterrent to the power of sin.

2. Police Officer and <u>Stop</u> <u>Sign</u> Method

This particular teaching suggests that, upon the first thought of temptation, we should visualize a police officer running up to us and holding a big "STOP" sign in front of our faces. This method is designed to help us understand that we should "stop" from indulging our flesh in sinful activities. I tried visualizing a police officer with a stop sign when thoughts of viewing pornography would enter my mind, when I was tempted to sit down and eat a whole pizza, or when I desired to get drunk. But the temptations were so powerful that I think I would have entirely disregarded even a real police officer to get to my sin.

3. <u>Regressive</u> Therapy

This theory states that the reason we are involved in certain activities today is because of some trauma or unfortunate events that happened to us at some point in the past. If we can go back and relive those events, our damaged emotions can be healed. I have previously spent many years reliving past events, trying to bring Jesus into the hard times, trying to right wrongs and fix mistakes, etc. Yet my involvement in pornography, drunkenness and overeating continued during this time.

4. Visualize <u>Emotional</u> Experience

This method tells us that temptation is a highly emotionally-charged experience. Therefore if, at the moment of temptation, we will visualize another highly emotionally charged experience, such as the birth of a child or the death of a parent, the second highly emotionally charged experience can overpower the first.

5. Sniffing <u>Ammonia</u>

This is a dangerous teaching which states that ammonia affects the brain waves and, when sniffed at the proper moment, will interrupt the temptation sequence of events. This particular theory fails to grasp the point that temptation affects the heart, not merely the brain waves (thoughts). We give in to sin because we want to, because we desire to, because our hearts long to do so, not merely because of certain spikes in brain activity. Thankfully, I never sniffed ammonia to try to be set free from sin.

6. "<u>Cut</u> <u>Back</u>" Principle

This principle teaches an addict to wean him or herself off the particular bad habit in which he or she is involved. I remember one counselor telling me to cut back from 20 pornographic movies per month to 18, and the next month to 16, and within a few years I'd be down to just 1 or 2. The following story is an illustration of the "cut back" or "wean off" principle.

TORONTO (Reuters) - Giving homeless alcoholics a regular supply of booze may improve their health and their behavior, the Canadian Medical Association Journal said in a study published on Tuesday.

Seventeen homeless adults, all with long and chronic histories of alcohol abuse, were allowed up to 15 glasses of wine or sherry a day -- a glass an hour from 7 a.m. to 10 p.m. -- in the Ottawa-based program, which started in 2002 and is continuing.

"The alcohol gets them in, builds the trust and then we have the opportunity to treat other medical diseases... It's about improving the quality of life." We are giving   alcohol   to those in bondage to alcohol, to "improve their quality of life."

Three of the 17 participants died during the program, succumbing to alcohol-related illnesses that might have killed them anyway, the study said.

All of the above principles fall short of the mark, as each one fails to grasp the truth that Jesus stated in Matthew 15:18-20:

> [18] But the things that come out of the mouth come from the heart, and these make a man unclean. [19] For out of the heart come evil thoughts, murder, adultery, sexual immorality, theft, false testimony, slander. [20] These are what make a man unclean; but eating with unwashed hands does not make him unclean.

Sin is first and foremost an issue of the <u>heart</u>. A heart cannot be changed by snapping the wrist, visualizing certain experiences, or by revisiting past events in our lives. A change of heart comes as a result of a person believing in and applying the message of the gospel through the work of the Holy Spirit in his or her life. (see Ezekiel 36:25-27).

Now let's consider the biblical method of freedom, the method a man would use to "cleanse himself," and thereby become a **Man of Honor**. We wish to focus on three important points. Like a three-legged stool, each point is important and necessary to a person finding freedom from habitual sin and to "not falling" to sinful habits.

The first point comes from Isaiah, chapter 53, and finds its New Testament counterpart in Matthew, chapter 5. Let's look at Isaiah 53 first, verses 4-8:

> [4] Surely he took up our infirmities and carried our sorrows, yet we considered him stricken by God, smitten by him, and afflicted. [5] But he was pierced for our transgressions, he was crushed for our iniquities; the punishment that brought us   peace was upon him, and by his wounds we are healed. [6] We all, like sheep, have gone astray, each of us has turned to his own way; and the LORD has laid on him the iniquity of us all. [7] He was oppressed and afflicted, yet he did not open his mouth; he was led like a lamb to the slaughter, and as a sheep before her shearers is silent, so he did not open his mouth. [8] By oppression and judgment he was taken

away. And who can speak of his descendants? For he was cut off from the land of the living; for the transgression of my people he was stricken.

This "Old Testament gospel," written 700 years B.C., is a clear portrayal of the sufferings, death, and resurrection of the Messiah. It states that this "suffering servant" (Isaiah 52:13-15) would "carry our infirmities and sorrows" (verse 4), that He would be "pierced for our transgressions" and "crushed for our iniquities" (verse 5). It states that He would take our punishment upon Himself, and that we would be healed by His wounds. (verse 5) As the passage culminates in the final act of the death of the Messiah on behalf of sinners, one particular phrase becomes important for our study. **Verse 8 tells us that Jesus Christ the Messiah was "<u>cut</u> <u>off</u> from the land of the living."**

Here we have displayed before us both God's abhorrence of sin, and also the extreme manner in which He dealt with it at the cross. God placed our sins on His Son; Jesus "became sin for us" (2 Corinthians 5:21), and then God "cut Him off." Like a surgeon dealing with a gangrened limb, God radically amputated His Son and "cut Him off" from the land of the living.

The manner in which God dealt with sin at the cross is also the manner in which God commands us to deal with sin. This same radical terminology is used when we come to dealing with sin in the New Testament.

Let's look at Matthew 5: 29-30:

> [29] If your right eye causes you to sin, gouge it out and throw it away. It is better for you to lose one part of your body than for your whole body to be thrown into hell. [30] And if your right hand causes you to sin, cut it off and throw it away. It is better for you to lose one part of your body than for your whole body to go into hell.

Again, we have placed before us a radical manner of dealing with sin. Quite the opposite of the "cut *back*" method, Scripture places before us the need to "cut *off*" all access to that which could cause us to sin. **A man of honor is one who takes sin <u>seriously</u> and deals with it <u>radically</u>.**

Now a word of explanation is needed here, in that Jesus Christ was not talking in a literal, physical sense in this passage. His instruction is not for us to dismember our bodies if we struggle with sin. Blind men and lame men still struggle with lust.

What Jesus is saying is that, if we find we are struggling with sin, we need to completely remove access to it, no matter how radical we must be in doing so.

The first biblical principle to finding freedom from sin is Radical <u>Amputation</u>.

When I first came to understand that the cross of Jesus Christ was a "radical amputation" of my sin, and that God commanded me to likewise "cut off" and "pluck out" all access to sin, I did the following things, which illustrate **some ways to apply the principle of radical amputation:**

1. I began **taking the TV out of my hotel room** when I went on layovers in the course of my job as a pilot. I can still remember the first time I unhooked and unplugged the TV and walked out the door of my hotel room with it. As I was walking down the hall, a housekeeper walked by me on the other side of the hallway, and stared at me with a very quizzical look on her face (as did my co-pilot when I knocked on his door and asked him to keep the TV in his room for the night). These experiences were somewhat embarrassing. But my pastor told me that, if I were not willing to be embarrassed, I would never be free. I continued to remove the TV from my hotel room for a full year.

2. I **gave away my notebook computer**. Since I had been accessing porn movies on the computer, I understood now that I was to radically amputate it, and gave it to my pastor. This required somewhat of a lifestyle change, as I had been using my computer to pay bills online, to do research for my job, and for other important purposes. But the visual image of a man plucking out his eye, or cutting off his hand, convinced me that even though there would be "pain," I must radically remove that which was causing me to stumble.

3. I **gave away my cell phone**, as I had been accessing 900 numbers with it in the past.

Now it is about this time that we usually get an objection, which goes like this: "Wait a minute, this all sounds so radical and extreme. I thought that, as Christians, we are to live balanced lives, that we are to be "normal" or "moderate;" that is, that we are to live life in a reasonable way."

To this objection I say, "I can agree with you. However, isn't it reasonable to be radical in destroying that which seeks to destroy you?" Jesus was clear in His instruction in Matthew 5 - we are to do "whatever it takes" to remove all access to sin.

Now, one word of caution is needed here. We are not those who would tear ourselves away from society and go live in caves. Nor do we believe that all technology is bad and to be avoided. No, we are to live *in* this world but not be *of* it. We are to be salt and light in this world, which means that we are to influence the world around us. We are not stating here that we cannot have TVs in our homes, that we cannot use the Internet, or that we must rid our lives of all entertainment and technology. No. What we are saying is simply this: if we are in *bondage* to sin, and we are getting *access* to areas that tempt us, then *those* areas must be removed for a time.

Many people have TVs and use the Internet without being involved in any habitual sin issues with them whatsoever. I am now able to leave the TV in my hotel room on layovers (and have done so for the past several years). I also have a computer with an Internet connection. So what we are stating is, that for a time, all access to that to which I am *in bondage* must be severed completely, so that I cannot get to it. A man without an eye cannot see that which would tempt him, and a man without a hand cannot get access to his flesh in order to gratify it. That is the point.

To illustrate this truth, let me mention a well-respected and much-loved pastor, John Piper of Bethlehem Baptist church in Minneapolis, Minnesota. Pastor Piper was diagnosed with prostate cancer in December of 2005. He wrote the following at the end of December:

"Before going with my wife, Noël, to consult in person with the doctor on December 29 about treatment options, I shared this news with the Bethlehem staff on Tuesday morning, December 27, and with the elders that evening. Both groups prayed over me for healing and for wisdom in the treatment choices that lie before us. These were sweet times before the throne of grace with much-loved colleagues.

All things considered, Noël and I believe that I should pursue the treatment called radical prostatectomy, which means the surgical removal of the prostate. We would ask you to pray that the surgery be completely successful in the removal of all cancer and freedom from possible side effects."

Imagine John and Noël Piper talking with the doctor and saying, "Yes, doctor, we have examined our treatment options and have elected for the surgery. However, we don't really want to go with the "radical" prostatectomy, we just want to remove *some* of the prostate for now. We want to have a "reasonable prostatectomy." The doctor would say, "John, why do you want to leave some of the cancerous, poisonous cells? If you leave any cancer cells, the cancer will kill you."

It is reasonable to be "<u>radical</u>" in destroying the sin that desires to destroy us. Or, to change analogies, if we leave the door to sin open one inch, the devil will drive a Mack truck through it. **Men of honor** radically amputate all access to sin, and slam the door shut to the evil one.

Our first biblical principle to finding freedom from life-dominating sin is **Radical Amputation.** Our second principle is found in John, chapter 6. Let us review verses 50 to 57:

[50] But here is the bread that comes down from heaven, which a man may eat and not die. [51] I am the living bread that came down from heaven. If anyone eats of this bread, he will live forever. This bread is my flesh, which I will give for the life of the world." [52] Then the Jews began to argue sharply among themselves, "How can this man give us his flesh to eat?" [53] Jesus said to them, "I tell you the truth, unless you eat the flesh of the Son of Man and drink his blood, you have no life in you. [54] Whoever eats my flesh and drinks my blood has eternal life, and I will raise him up at the last day. [55] For my flesh is real food and my blood is real drink. [56] Whoever eats my flesh and drinks my blood remains in me, and I in him.

⁵⁷ Just as the living Father sent me and I live because of the Father, so the one who feeds on me will live because of me (John 6:50-57).

In this passage, **Jesus makes the assertion that, in order to live forever, we must <u>feed</u> on Him.** This is an odd statement to be sure, and we must take time to understand the meaning. Again, Jesus was obviously not speaking literally, as if to invite us to take a bite out of His arm, or to in any other way gnaw on His flesh. Rather, He is speaking spiritually, inviting us to derive *life from His death*; that is, to learn how to enjoy the benefits of the cross by appropriating His death into our lives.

In other words, we are to feast our souls on the reality that we are forgiven through Jesus' death, that we are reconciled to God through the cross, that we are accepted in the Beloved. We are to feed on the following truths:
- We are redeemed from sin through Jesus' blood
- We are free from bondage through the cross
- We have escaped the wrath of God because Jesus took it all upon Himself.

These truths are to nourish our souls and to fill us up. (See 1Timothy 4:6)

This second principle of freedom, then, is called Radical <u>Appropriation</u>.

When we consider this truth, we can understand why it is so important to our freedom. We have just cut off and totally removed all access to that with which we previously spent an inordinate amount of time and thought and energy. Nature abhors a vacuum, and we are now open and susceptible to other addictions, or to returning to previous sin patterns. It becomes imperative, then, that we replace and refill the void (created by the removal of habitual sin) with Christ and with the Word of God, so that we will not be empty, open, and exposed to further onslaughts of temptation.

Following is a very scary reminder in Luke 11:24-27, of the dangers of not radically appropriating Jesus Christ.

> ²⁴ "When an evil spirit comes out of a man, it goes through arid places seeking rest and does not find it. Then it says, 'I will return to the house I left.' ²⁵ When it arrives, it finds the house swept clean and put in order. ²⁶ Then it goes and takes seven other spirits more wicked than itself, and they go in and live there. And the final condition of that man is worse than the first." ²⁷ As Jesus was saying these things, a woman in the crowd called out, "Blessed is the mother who gave you birth and nursed you."

We find here that the man in the passage above was "clean" yet he was "empty." And because of this "empty" condition, he was susceptible to all manner of evil, and his condition in the end was worse than before he cleaned up his house.

Such is the case with men who are involved in pornography, drunkenness, immorality, gambling, or overeating. When they decide to "clean house," if they don't rapidly begin to appropriate the Word of God and learn how to feast on Jesus Christ, they can go from bad to worse in a hurry. We have seen men who were enslaved to porn employ radical amputation and make it so that they cannot get to that which had enslaved them. But if they failed to turn to the Lord, to soak in His Word, to apply His truth, they quickly turned to alcohol and became drunks, to gambling and became addicted, or to other life-dominating sins.

The first biblical principle to finding freedom from sin is **Radical Amputation**.

The second principle of freedom is called **Radical Appropriation**.

The third principle of freedom is Radical <u>Accountability.</u>

Gary Inrig, in <u>Life in His Body</u>, shared the following story: "Several years ago, two students graduated from the Chicago-Kent College of Law. The highest ranking student in the class was a blind man named Overton and, when he received his honor, he insisted that half the credit should go to his friend, Kaspryzak. They had met one another in school when the armless Mr. Kaspryzak had guided the blind Mr. Overton down a flight of stairs. This acquaintance ripened into friendship and a beautiful example of interdependence. The blind man carried the books which the armless man read aloud in their common study, and thus the individual deficiency of each was compensated for by the other.

"After their graduation, they planned to practice law together. No believer is complete by himself, we are to minister to one another, as a family."

We find the third principle in Ecclesiastes 4:9-12. Let us look there just now:

> [9] Two are better than one, because they have a good return for their work: [10] If one falls down, his friend can help him up. But pity the man who falls and has no one to help him up! [11] Also, if two lie down together, they will keep warm. But how can one keep warm alone? [12] Though one may be overpowered, two can defend themselves. A cord of three strands is not quickly broken.

Ecclesiastes 4:9-12 presents to us the value of walking <u>together</u> with another fellow traveler, and of enjoying ongoing <u>accountability</u> with one another.

Verse 9 speaks of **spiritual fruit**. Two are better than one because they are more fruitful than one would be alone. They have a good return for their work.

Verse 10 speaks of **spiritual restoration**. If two are walking together and one falls, his friend can help him up.

Verse 11 speaks of **spiritual zeal**. Two together can help keep each other "on fire" for the Lord, that is, keep each other warm.

Verse 12 speaks of **spiritual protection**. Two can defend themselves against the attacks of the enemy.

The principle of **Radical <u>Accountability</u>** teaches us to find a partner to walk with so that we might enjoy the benefits of producing more together than we would alone, of helping one another with stumbles or falls, with encouraging each other in our devotion to the Lord, and of helping to protect one another from the attacks of our enemy.

Typically, most men are loners! We think that being manly is being independent. We don't need anything or anyone, that's why we don't ask for directions. Real men do it themselves.

Not men of honor. A real man of honor is dependent on God, and the more dependent he is, the more mature and the more honorable he is. A real man of honor is also dependant on his brothers in Christ. We need each other, and it is our call and duty to hold one another accountable. We are a band of brothers!

The military is famous for the phrase "no man left behind." The idea is that you do not leave a soldier on the battlefield; he is your brother. How much more should we be concerned for our brothers in Christ who are caught in life-dominating sin!

Lewis Timberlake, in *Timberlake Monthly*, related this personal story:

"While on a tour of California's giant sequoias, the guide pointed out that the sequoia tree has roots just barely below the surface. "That's impossible!" I exclaimed. "I'm a country boy, and I know that if the roots don't grow deep into the earth, strong winds will blow the trees over." 'Not sequoia trees,' said the guide. 'They grow only in groves and their roots intertwine under the surface of the earth. So, when the strong winds come, they hold each other up.'

"There's a lesson here. In a sense, people are like the giant sequoias. Family, friends, neighbors, the church body and other groups should be havens so that when the strong winds of life blow, these people can serve as reinforcement and can strive together to hold each other up."

Here are some helpful methods of maintaining accountability when desiring to come out of habitual sin, listed in the form of "do's" and "don'ts."

Do...

- Share <u>openly</u> and honestly
- Take the <u>initiative</u> in the relationship. Provide daily reports of progress through email, phone, meeting, etc. without your partner having to contact you

- Provide your <u>spouse</u> with access to your accountability partner, so that he or she can contact the partner with any questions/concerns
- Follow their <u>biblical</u> counsel. Receive their input
- <u>Thank</u> them

Do not...

- Lie to your accountability <u>partner</u>
- Treat your accountability partner as your savior to keep you out of sin, or as a <u>janitor</u> to continually sweep up your messes, or as a priest for continual confession of sin, as a <u>crutch</u> to lean and depend upon, or as a <u>babysitter</u> to watch over you every minute.
- Blame them if you fall instead of accepting <u>responsibility</u>
- Give your accountability partner a hard time, since they are there to <u>help</u> you

[21] If a man cleanses himself from the latter, he will be an instrument for noble purposes, made holy, useful to the Master and prepared to do any good work. [22] Flee the evil desires of youth, and pursue righteousness, faith, love and peace, along with those who call on the Lord out of a pure heart (2 Timothy 2:21-22).

A Man of Honor **radically amputates** all access to impurity. A Man of Honor **radically appropriates** the Lord Jesus Christ, immersing himself in and applying the Scripture that he reads. A Man of Honor **maintains accountability** relationships with others in the body of Christ.

Bill, the attorney, said, "I had tried psychological counseling, the 'professionals' who mainly tried to teach me how I got involved in pornography. I tried an anonymous group, and I tried various techniques I read about on the Internet. But it wasn't until I saw these three principles from the Bible, that I understood clearly what I had to do. That very night I canceled my cable TV subscription and closed two accounts at porn video stores. Whenever I would normally have turned to pornography, I now began to seek the Lord, to read His Word and pray, and to try to apply what I was reading. I also asked my friend to be my accountability partner and, for a whole year, I sent him daily reports as to my progress. I'm sure he is glad to finally not be getting so many of them, but I needed that type of intense accountability, initially. I truly do love the freedom that Jesus died to give me, and the new life I have in Him. We are even bringing the '**Men of Honor**' series into our church this coming month, and I am looking forward to seeing other men becoming Men of Honor, also."

Men of Honor Session Two Worksheet

False Solutions the world offers today:

1. _____ _____ Method

2. Police Officer and _____ _____ Method

3. _____ Therapy

4. Visualize _____ Experience

5. Sniffing _____

6. _____ _____ Principle

[18] But the things that come out of the mouth come from the heart, and these make a man 'unclean.' [19] For out of the heart come evil thoughts, murder, adultery, sexual immorality, theft, false testimony, slander. [20] These are what make a man 'unclean'; but eating with unwashed hands does not make him 'unclean'" (Matthew 15:18-20).

Sin is first and foremost an issue of the _____.

[4] Surely he took up our infirmities and carried our sorrows, yet we considered him stricken by God, smitten by him, and afflicted. [5] But he was pierced for our transgressions, he was crushed for our iniquities; the punishment that brought us peace was upon him, and by his wounds we are healed. [6] We all, like sheep, have gone astray, each of us has turned to his own way; and the LORD has laid on him the iniquity of us all. [7] He was oppressed and afflicted, yet he did not open his mouth; he was led like a lamb to the slaughter, and as a sheep before her shearers is silent, so he did not open his mouth. [8] By oppression and judgment he was taken away. And who can speak of his descendants? For he was cut off from the land of the living; for the transgression of my people he was stricken (Isaiah 53:4-8).

Verse 8 tells us that Jesus Christ the Messiah was " _____
from the land of the living."

[29] If your right eye causes you to sin, gouge it out and throw it away. It is better for you to lose one part of your body than for your whole body to be thrown into hell. [30] And if your right hand causes you to sin, cut it off and throw it away. It is better for you to lose one part of your body than for your whole body to go into hell (Matthew 5:29-30).

A Man of Honor is one who takes sin _____ and deals with it
_____.

The first biblical principle to finding freedom from sin is Radical
_____.

Some ways to apply the principle of radical amputation include:

      1.

      2.

      3.

It is _____ to be "radical" in destroying the _____ that desires to destroy us.

[50] But here is the bread that comes down from heaven, which a man may eat and not die. [51] I am the living bread that came down from heaven. If anyone eats of this bread, he will live forever. This bread is my flesh, which I will give for the life of the world." [52] Then the Jews began to argue sharply among themselves, "How can this man give us his flesh to eat?" [53] Jesus said to them, "I tell you the truth, unless you eat the flesh of the Son of Man and drink his blood, you have no life in you. [54] Whoever eats my flesh and drinks my blood has eternal life, and I will raise him up at the last day. [55] For my flesh is real food and my blood is real drink. [56] Whoever eats my flesh and drinks my blood remains in me, and I in him. [57] Just as the living Father sent me and I live because of the Father, so the one who feeds on me will live because of me (John 6:50-57).

Jesus makes the assertion that, in order to live forever, we must _____ on Him.

This second principle of freedom is called Radical _____.

[24] "When an evil spirit comes out of a man, it goes through arid places seeking rest and does not find it. Then it says, 'I will return to the house I left.' [25] When it arrives, it finds the house swept clean and put in order. [26] Then it goes and takes seven other spirits more wicked than itself, and they go in and live there. And the final condition of that man is worse than the first." [27] As Jesus was saying these things, a woman in the crowd called out, "Blessed is the mother who gave you birth and nursed you" (Luke 11:24-27).

[9] Two are better than one, because they have a good return for their work: [10] If one falls down, his friend can help him up. But pity the man who falls and has no one to help him up! [11] Also, if two lie down together, they will keep warm. But how can one keep warm

alone? [12] Though one may be overpowered, two can defend themselves. A cord of three strands is not quickly broken (Ecclesiastes 4:9-12).

Ecclesiastes 4:9-12 presents to us the value of walking _____ with another fellow traveler, and of enjoying ongoing _____ with   one   another.

Our third principle is Radical _____.

Here are some helpful methods of maintaining accountability when desiring to come out of habitual sin, listed in the form of "do's" and "don'ts."

Do...

1. Share_____ and honestly
2. Take the _____ in the relationship. Provide daily reports of progress through email, phone, meeting, etc. without your partner having to contact you
3. Provide your _____ with access to your accountability partner, so that he or she can contact the partner with any questions/concerns
4. Follow their _____ counsel. Receive their input
5. _____ them

Do not...

1. Lie to your accountability _____
2. Treat your accountability partner as your savior to keep you out of sin, or as a _____ to continually sweep up your messes, or as a priest for continual confession of sin, as a _____ to lean and depend upon, or as a _____ to watch over you every minute.
3. Blame them if you fall instead of accepting _____
4. Give your accountability partner a hard time, since they are there to _____ you.

[21] If a man cleanses himself from the latter, he will be an instrument for noble purposes, made holy, useful to the Master and prepared to do any good work. [22] Flee the evil desires of youth, and pursue righteousness, faith, love and peace, along with those who call on the Lord out of a pure heart (2 Timothy 2:21-22).

Men of Honor Meetings—Session Two
Discussion Questions

(Main Session - Matthew 15:18-20, Isaiah 53:4-8; Matthew 5:29-30, John 6:50-57; Luke 11:24-27, Ecclesiastes 4:9-12, 2 Timothy 2:21-22; Small Groups - James 1:19-21; 1 Corinthians 5:6-8)

Question 1. In light of Matthew 5:29-30, why is it important to be radical in fighting against sin? Why does the "weaning from sin" principle, as taught by the world, not work?

Question 2. Which two of the three principles of freedom are found in James 1:19-22? Why is the implementation of both of these truths important to our freedom?

Question 3. Please read 1 Corinthians 5:6-8. How does this passage teach two out of three foundational truths to freedom from habitual sin?

Question 4. According to 1 Corinthians 5:7, what motivation does Paul provide for removing all sin and wickedness from our lives? Why is this compelling and urgent?

Question 5. Please read 2 Timothy 2:20-21. According to this passage, upon what is being a "man of honor" dependent? What four blessings are listed to those who will cleanse themselves?

Question 6. Please read through Ecclesiastes 4:9-12. Please discuss the importance of accountability, and of having a brother with whom to walk. What are the dangers listed in being "alone?"

Question 7. Application time. Have you radically amputated all access to that which has caused you to stumble? Are you "getting rid of all moral filth"? Are you "removing all the old yeast"?

Men of Honor — Session Three
Repentance Versus Remorse

Welcome to our third session in the **Men of Honor** Series. I'm very thankful to be sharing with you, my brothers, and walking with you in the learning and application of Scripture. Let's open our Bibles to 2 Timothy, chapter 2, as we look forward to what God has in store for us in this session.

By way of review, in the first session we studied John, chapter 4, and we noted that **those who drink from sin waters will "thirst again" which is the biblical term for "addiction."** We also noted that to find our satisfaction in Jesus Christ is to have our spiritual thirst quenched, so that we do not need to search for other sources of satisfaction. We saw that drinking the pure, Living Water of Jesus Christ quenches our thirst, and makes us pure, as well. **Men of Honor are those who drink deeply of Jesus** and therefore do not thirst for pornography, illicit relationships, alcohol, cigarettes or any other area of sinful bondage.

In the second session, we studied the false solutions the world offers to help people out of sin, and then we noted the three biblical principles of freedom. We read in the Bible about **"radical amputation,"** the cutting off and plucking out of all avenues through which sin might enter. We studied **"radical appropriation"** which means to feed on the Lord Jesus Christ, applying the Scriptures to our lives, and deriving spiritual nourishment from His death. Finally, we studied the need for **"radical accountability"**, which means to be transparent with our spouse and other brothers and sisters, providing daily accounting of our spiritual condition so that the devil has no place to hide in our lives. **Men of Honor** are those who remove all sources of stumbling from their lives, who feast their souls on Christ, and who walk in openness and transparency with their families and brothers and sisters in the Lord.

In this session, we want to discuss a principle so important that, if applied to the life, will secure freedom from all life-dominating sin. This session is called "Repentance Vs. Remorse" and we want to study the Bible to learn and apply its teachings about this extremely important topic.

It is said that one of the most notorious murderers throughout history would pray and ask forgiveness each time he would take a life. This, however, is not genuine repentance but merely remorse, as we will study in this session.

To illustrate the difference between remorse and repentance, Rubel Shelly recounts the following story:

Some Christians seem to have missed the significance of repentance *for the new life to which God calls his children. Grace not only offers pardon but also demands and produces transformation.*

"But that wasn't the case with me," protests someone. "I genuinely repented of my past when I came to Christ, but I just can't break away from pornography (or cursing or fornication or alcohol)." That is distinctly possible. In order to defeat sin, however, one must go beyond remorse and sincere determination to turn away from evil. He or she must take an additional step of "burning the boats."

When Julius Caesar landed on the shores of England with his well-armed legions, he simultaneously made a bold and decisive move to guarantee the success of his campaign. He marched his men to the edge of the Cliffs of Dover and ordered them to look down at the ships that had brought them across the channel. Every one of them was ablaze! General Caesar had cut off the possibility of a pullback. Now that his soldiers were unable to return to the continent, there was nothing left for them to do but advance and conquer. And that is precisely what they did".   (www.sermonillustrator.org)

Let's pray together and ask for God's help to understand His Word, and to apply what He reveals in it.

Now let's examine 2 Timothy 2:22-26:

> [22] Flee the evil desires of youth, and pursue righteousness, faith, love and peace, along with those who call on the Lord out of a pure heart. [23] Don't have anything to do with foolish and stupid arguments, because you know they produce quarrels. [24] And the Lord's servant must not quarrel; instead, he must be kind to everyone, able to teach, not resentful. [25] Those who oppose him he must gently instruct, in the hope that God will grant them repentance leading them to a knowledge of the truth, [26] and that they will

come to their senses and escape from the trap of the devil, who has taken them captive to do his will.

These verses follow the passage we have chosen for our theme passage, which states, "If anyone cleanses himself…he will be a vessel of honor." In this passage, Paul instructs Timothy how to minister to various people. **He states, first of all, that Timothy's own life must be lived in <u>purity</u>.** He was to "flee the evil desires of youth" and to "pursue righteousness, faith, love and peace" along with those who call on the Lord "out of a pure heart."

Secondly, Paul tells Timothy not to <u>argue</u> and quarrel with others, but rather be kind to all, gently instructing those who oppose him, and not to be resentful. Paul's stated reason that Timothy must not argue and quarrel over the truth is "in the hope that God will grant them repentance, leading them to knowledge of the truth, and that they will come to their senses and escape from the trap of the devil, who has taken them captive to do his will."

In this portion of Scripture, we learn an important truth about repentance. **First, we see that repentance is a <u>gift</u> of God**. Timothy was not to argue with those who are argumentative in hopes that God would *grant* them repentance. Timothy was not to argue, for it is God Who gives ears to hear and a heart to turn from sin. Repentance is a **sovereign gift** of God, given to whomever He wills.

This same truth is taught in Acts 11:18:

> When they heard this, they had no further objections and praised God, saying, "So then, God has granted even the Gentiles repentance unto life."

It is important to understand that it is in God's control, and it is His decision to bestow the gift of repentance on whomever He desires. Therefore, we must seek God for a heart to turn away from sin if we desire to find freedom from "addiction." Repentance does not come from man. It does not come based upon any decision man makes, nor any action on his part. **Repentance is <u>initiated</u> by God, is a gift of God, and comes from His <u>grace</u>.** Genuine repentance comes as I see my wretched and hopeless condition in sin, as I see the perfect Solution in Jesus Christ, and as I seek the Lord for forgiveness of my sins and ask Him to turn me from them.

This is what David did in Psalm 51 as he prayed for God to have mercy on him, and blot out all his transgressions (verse 1), as he prayed that God would cleanse him (verse 7) and create in him a pure heart (verse 10). This is David seeking for repentance; that is, he sought God to give him a heart that was pure and a life that was clean.

So the first point about repentance is to acknowledge that it is a gift of God, and that it comes by His grace, and that God gives it to whomever He pleases. When we desire to be free of any sin, we first seek the Lord for grace, we petition Him to make a change in us at the core of our being, and we ask Him for mercy and grace to repent of sin. **Men of**

Honor are those who, when they recognize sin in their own lives, do as David did and **plead with God for a new <u>heart</u>, a right spirit, a <u>willing</u> spirit.**

Now, it is important to understand that even though repentance is a sovereign gift of God, each person is responsible before God for repenting of sin and believing in Jesus. Acts 17:30 states it this way, "In the past God overlooked such ignorance, but now he commands all people everywhere to repent." This tells us that no one may use the sovereign grace of God as an excuse to continue in sin. We've heard people say, "Well God did not give me the gift of repentance, so until He does, I will persist in my ways." No, **God has commanded all people everywhere to <u>repent</u>, and holds us <u>responsible</u> for doing so.**

Now one might say, "I did repent when I became a Christian." But we are talking about ongoing repentance here. As a person grows in Christian maturity, he will become more and more aware of his sin and how his sin offends God. A man of honor is not a man who claims to be without sin, but a man who recognizes his sin often, and is in the habit of repenting before the Lord. Christians are to be "believing believers" and "repenting repenters."

The fact that God commands all people to repent, yet must give the gift of repentance to us, is one of the great mysteries in Scripture, and delving into this mystery is beyond the scope of our meetings. Suffice it to say that both concepts are true, and both are helpful to those who truly desire to be free from sin. So when we desire to be free from sin, we seek God for a heart of change, and then **we repent**. We turn away from sin and we turn to the Lord, and by so doing, we acknowledge that God has worked in our hearts and lives to turn us from sin by His grace.

Now let us examine two final points about repentance that may help us to better understand the nature of it. First, let us look at 2 Corinthians 7:8-13:

> [8] Even if I caused you sorrow by my letter, I do not regret it. Though I did regret it—I see that my letter hurt you, but only for a little while-- [9] yet now I am happy, not because you were made sorry, but because your sorrow led you to repentance. For you became sorrowful as God intended and so were not harmed in any way by us. [10] Godly sorrow brings repentance that leads to salvation and leaves no regret, but worldly sorrow brings death. [11] See what this godly sorrow has produced in you: what earnestness, what eagerness to clear yourselves, what indignation, what alarm, what longing, what concern, what readiness to see justice done. At every point you have proved yourselves to be innocent in this matter. [12] So even though I wrote to you, it was not on account of the one who did the wrong or of the injured party, but rather that before God you could see for yourselves how devoted to us you are. [13] By all this we are encouraged. In addition to our own encouragement, we were especially delighted to see how happy Titus was, because his spirit has been refreshed by all of you.

36

Did you notice how many times Paul uses the term "sorrow," "sorry" or "sorrowful" in the first three verses? I counted seven times, which is more than two times per verse. And he contrasts "godly sorrow" with "worldly sorrow." **The second point about repentance is that repentance is preceded by <u>godly</u> sorrow.**

It is important to note that godly sorrow leads to genuine repentance (verse 9). While worldly sorrow leaves one in sin, which leads to death, godly sorrow is that condition of having a broken heart; not over getting caught, but over the sin itself. It is looking at my life of selfishness and experiencing a brokenness, true contrition, and real sorrow. It is also looking at the sufferings of Christ, His blood shed on the cross, His infinite love displayed for hardened rebels, and experiencing a heart-sorrow that reaches to the very depths of my being.

David experienced this brokenness as he sought God for change:

> ¹⁶ You do not delight in sacrifice, or I would bring it; you do not take pleasure in burnt offerings. ¹⁷ The sacrifices of God are a broken spirit; a broken and contrite heart, O God, you will not despise (Psalm 51:16-17).

David was made sorry for his sins, indeed was brokenhearted over them. This was godly sorrow that led to genuine repentance and freedom from further habitual sins.

The determining factor of whether the sorrow we have is "worldly" or "godly" is whether or not it leads us to truly <u>repent</u>. You see, I lived for many years with worldly sorrow, that is, with mere remorse. I would sin in the darkness, then feel really bad that I couldn't be stronger, and determine not to do the sin again. But when temptation came, I was already so weak from previous falls that I would fall again. Then I would feel bad again, vow again to stop, and then watch the heat of temptation melt away all my promises to do better. My sorrow was not genuine; it did not lead to real repentance.

For me, what it took was to radically amputate the source of temptation and sin. Then as I stepped out of the darkness and into the light, I began to see myself through God's eyes, and through the eyes of my spouse. I recognized that I had previously been blinded to the wretchedness of sin, and I was living in pride and self-centeredness. Only when I came into the light did I begin to experience godly sorrow, as well as the humbling that comes with it. When I saw myself in the light, I looked awfully bad, very self-absorbed, and totally depraved. I cried for literally months on end over who I was and what I had become. I also began looking intently at the cross, and seeing the intense suffering of Jesus Christ for my sins, and that broke my heart as well. This was a time of true brokenness of heart by God, and a yearning to be free on my part. I was unknowingly doing as James commands:

> ⁸ Come near to God and he will come near to you. Wash your hands, you sinners, and purify your hearts, you double-minded. ⁹ Grieve, mourn and wail. Change your laughter to mourning and your joy to gloom. ¹⁰ Humble yourselves before the Lord, and he will lift you up (James 4:8-10).

37

The first point about repentance is that **repentance is a gift of God.** The second point is that genuine **repentance is preceded by godly sorrow**, by being brokenhearted over sin.

The final point about repentance is that it is a real turning <u>from</u> sin, and turning <u>to</u> God. Repentance is not merely a 90-degree turn away from sin, for that condition leaves us susceptible to going back to sin, or to turning to another sin. No, real repentance is a full turn away from sin and to the living God. Notice how this truth is stated in Romans 6:20-22:

> **20** When you were slaves to sin, you were free from the control of righteousness. **21** What benefit did you reap at that time from the things you are now ashamed of? Those things result in death! **22** But now that you have been set free from sin and have become slaves to God, the benefit you reap leads to holiness, and the result is eternal life.

The people Paul was writing to in Romans had gone from being sin-slaves to becoming "Son-slaves." They were previously enslaved to sin; now they had been set free and had become "slaves of God." This is repentance. It is a full 180-degree turn from sin and to the Lord. Another example of genuine repentance is in Acts 26:18:

> (I am sending you) to open their eyes and turn them from darkness to light, and from the power of Satan to God, so that they may receive forgiveness of sins and a place among those who are sanctified by faith in me.

This, again, is real repentance. It is people who turn:

- **from <u>darkness</u> to light**
- **from the power of Satan to <u>God</u>**

I remember clearly when God worked in my heart, giving me grace to turn from sin to Christ. I understood that Jesus was the Light, and I wanted to be enveloped in the Light so as to be truly finished with the deeds of darkness. I understood that in God's presence there was protection from the assaults of the evil one, and so I wanted to live in His presence. This was a time of true heartbroken repentance and finding real life in Christ.

Men of Honor are those who seek the Lord for godly sorrow, who ask Him for the gift of repentance, who turn away from sin in all its forms, and who turn to Jesus to become His happy captive. This is repentance. This is life. And there is wonderful and enjoyable freedom when we repent and pour our hearts out to the Lord.

On Day 14 of the Door of Hope course at Setting Captives Free at www.settingcaptivesfree.com, a student named Tim wrote the following:

"As I read this lesson I realize that God has granted me the qualities of repentance. When I hear things on the television about homosexuality being glorified, I no longer laugh and enjoy the show, but rather I feel remorse and sorrow for those who are being fed the lie by Satan that this is acceptable. I am now offended by these types of concepts imbedded into mainstream media. I have no desire to be entertained by these things. God has given me a distaste for sin and immorality that I did not previously have. I feel true heart-sorrow over my own life of sin. I also feel sorrow for those who are so far from God and His truth about homosexuality, and the fact that the lies of Satan are becoming tolerable and accepted, and no longer taboo in our society. This worldly acceptance of homosexuality will only make it harder for those in true spiritual darkness to come into the spiritual light."

Notice Tim's repentance here. We know that this godly sorrow and genuine repentance is coming to Tim as a gift of God, given by His grace. Tim, an ex-homosexual is now becoming a **Man of Honor** as he cleanses himself, repents of his sin, and begins to enjoy the Light of truth.

It is my heart's desire that any man here today who is in the "sin/repent, sin/repent" cycle, would seek the Lord earnestly for a broken heart, and for the godly sorrow that leads to repentance, and that true repentance would be evidenced by a thorough turn from sin and to the Lord. My heart's burden is to see someone here today who has been failing and falling, who has been stumbling and sinning, begin to ask God for grace to turn from sin. Out of love for you, I want to see you become sorrowful for a time, hurting over sin, broken-hearted and humbled. May you "become sorrowful as God intended" (2 Corinthians 7:9) that you might repent of sin, and then live in the joy of the Lord for the rest of your life.

Men of Honor – Session Three Worksheet

Those who drink from sin waters will _____ _____, which is the biblical term for "addiction."

Men of Honor are those who _____ deeply of Jesus.

[22] Flee the evil desires of youth, and pursue righteousness, faith, love and peace, along with those who call on the Lord out of a pure heart. [23] Don't have anything to do with foolish and stupid arguments, because you know they produce quarrels. [24] And the Lord's servant must not quarrel; instead, he must be kind to everyone, able to teach, not resentful. [25] Those who oppose him he must gently instruct, in the hope that God will grant them repentance leading them to a knowledge of the truth, [26] and that they will come to their senses and escape from the trap of the devil, who has taken them captive to do his will (2 Timothy 2:22-26).

Paul states, first of all, that Timothy's own life must be lived in _____.

Secondly, Paul tells Timothy not to _____ and quarrel with others.

Above, we see that repentance is a _____ of God.

When they heard this, they had no further objections and praised God, saying, "So then, God has granted even the Gentiles repentance unto life" (Acts 11:18).

Repentance is _____ by God, is a gift of God, and comes from His _____.

Men of Honor are those who plead with God for a new _____, a right spirit, a _____ spirit.

God has commanded all people everywhere to _____, and holds us _____ for doing so.

[8] Even if I caused you sorrow by my letter, I do not regret it. Though I did regret it--I see that my letter hurt you, but only for a little while-- [9] yet now I am happy, not because you were made sorry, but because your sorrow led you to repentance. For you became sorrowful as God intended and so were not harmed in any way by us. [10] Godly sorrow brings repentance that leads to salvation and leaves no regret, but worldly sorrow brings death. [11] See what this godly sorrow has produced in you: what earnestness, what eagerness to clear yourselves, what indignation, what alarm, what longing, what concern, what readiness to see justice done. At every point you have proved yourselves to be

innocent in this matter. [12] So even though I wrote to you, it was not on account of the one who did the wrong or of the injured party, but rather that before God you could see for yourselves how devoted to us you are. [13] By all this we are encouraged. In addition to our own encouragement, we were especially delighted to see how happy Titus was, because his spirit has been refreshed by all of you (2 Corinthians 7:8-13).

The second point about repentance is that repentance is preceded by _____ sorrow.

[16] You do not delight in sacrifice, or I would bring it; you do not take pleasure in burnt offerings. [17] The sacrifices of God are a broken spirit; a broken and contrite heart, O God, you will not despise (Psalm 51:16-17).

The determining factor of whether the sorrow we have is "worldly" or "godly" is whether or not it leads us to truly _____.

[8] Come near to God and he will come near to you. Wash your hands, you sinners, and purify your hearts, you double-minded. [9] Grieve, mourn and wail. Change your laughter to mourning and your joy to gloom. [10] Humble yourselves before the Lord, and he will lift you up (James 4:8-10).

The final point about repentance is that it is a real turning _____ sin, and turning _____ God.

[20] When you were slaves to sin, you were free from the control of righteousness. [21] What benefit did you reap at that time from the things you are now ashamed of? Those things result in death! [22] But now that you have been set free from sin and have become slaves to God, the benefit you reap leads to holiness, and the result is eternal life. (Romans 6:20-22).

to open their eyes and turn them from darkness to light, and from the power of Satan to God, so that they may receive forgiveness of sins and a place among those who are sanctified by faith in me (Acts 26:18).

This, again, is real repentance. It is people who turn:

- From _____ to light
- From the power of Satan to _____.

Men of Honor — Session Three
Discussion Questions

(Main Session - 2 Timothy 2:22-26, Acts 11:18, 2 Corinthians 7:8-13, Psalms 51:16-17, James 4:8-10, Romans 6:20-22, Acts 26:18; Small Groups - Acts 26:15-18, 2 Timothy 2:24-26, Matthew 3:8.)

Question 1. Please examine Acts 26:15-18. In this passage of Scripture, how is repentance defined?

Question 2. According to Acts 26:15-18, what are the conditions of one who has not yet repented?

Question 3. In Acts 26:15-18, what are the stated benefits of repentance?

Question 4. Please examine 2 Timothy 2:24-26. What are the conditions of one who has not repented?

Question 5. According to 2 Timothy 2:24-26, how, specifically, was Timothy to treat and interact with those who were trapped in sin?

Question 6. According to 2 Timothy 2:24-26, what are the stated benefits of repentance?

Question 7. What does Matthew 3:8 tell us about genuine repentance?

Men of Honor — Session Four
Walking in the Light

Let's open our Bibles to John, chapter 3, as we begin our final session.

Thank you for coming back to this, our fourth session in the **Men of Honor** series. It is good to be able to study the Bible and learn from God how to be **Men of Honor**, for His glory.

And really, this subject and study for men is extremely important to the church today. I want to begin with a quote by David Murrow. In his book, titled "Why Men Hate Going to Church," he wrote,

"The movement of Christianity across South America is a movement of women, and I think it's got a shelf life of 2-3 generations before all the men are gone (from the church). I think it is setting the stage for Islam, and that Islam will be wildly popular in South America. **Islam is the fastest-growing <u>religion</u> in the world. Why? Because it attracts <u>men</u>.** *If men continue to turn away (from the church) as they are, I don't think there is any doubt that Islam will be the dominant religion in our nation within a few hundred years."*

So, what will it take to **stem the tide of men _leaving_ the church**, and women *leading* the church? I believe it is correct to say that **it will take men finding freedom from the grip of <u>sin</u>, men taking seriously the admonition to <u>cleanse</u> themselves, men truly becoming Men of <u>Honor</u>!**

Right now, as we begin this final session, I want you to come with me into the secret life of a "Christian" porn addict (we could substitute "drug addict," one who drinks excessively, overeats, or gambles, etc). He may have the appearance of being a spiritual man. He usually has many winsome qualities about him. He may teach Sunday school, or be an elder or even a pastor. In the business world, he may be successful and his family might have the outward appearance of being a loving family.

But despite the appearances, if you could be invisible and follow this man around in his life, you would see that he not only has his external, public life, but he also has a secret, hidden life. You might see him carefully arranging his schedule so as to make time to view pornography, or to arrange a secret liaison. You might see him rushing in to private places for the purpose of gratifying the lusts of his flesh. You might see him viewing more and more bizarre forms of porn with each passing year and each passing decade. You would see him being very careful to hide and protect this secret life, allowing nobody in, and guarding it from being discovered.

And even worse, if you could somehow get into the mind of a Christian porn addict, you would discover a virtual plethora of stored memories; his mind is literally a gallery of porn images with sexual scenarios constantly playing on the "Real Player" of his mind. And yet his virtual porn gallery is hidden from you and me; it is a secret that only he knows about - and his wife, if he is married. Oh, he may think it is hidden from his wife but, **because of the oneness of <u>marriage</u>, what happens in the husband's life affects his <u>wife</u>**, whether or not either one is aware of it.

This man has two lives, and he exercises the greatest care to ensure these two worlds of his never collide, that there is no intersection point whatsoever. He has an outer and public life and also an inner, hidden and secret life.

Setting Captives Free course member Jeff wrote: *"I can remember closing all the doors, pulling down the shades on the windows, drawing the curtains, turning off all lights in the house, and then, only after everything was dark, did I sit at the computer for my time of sinning in pornography and self-gratification."*

I lived in these two separate worlds for several years, carefully guarding my secret and hidden life so that I would not be found out. For 15 years, I lived in fear of man, in fear of discovery, and in fear of getting caught. I was like the man Jesus describes in John chapter 3 verses 19-20:

> [19] This is the verdict: Light has come into the world, but men loved darkness instead of light because their deeds were evil. [20] Everyone who does evil hates the light, and will not come into the light for fear that his deeds will be exposed (John 3:19-20).

Men may use all types of logical arguments as to why they aren't Christians or why they don't go to church. They may make statements, such as, "Oh, well, I just think that organized religion is corrupt," or "They are just all a bunch of hypocrites," or "They just want my money." But do you know what may be at the root of all these fine-sounding arguments? The reason may be the fear of discovery and the fear of exposure. He "will not come into the light for fear that his deeds will be exposed." He fears that his worlds will collide, causing a great explosion, and that he won't survive. He fears his secret life will be laid bare, that his evil deeds will be exposed, and he fears losing that in which he delights and finds pleasure.

A CNN special featured the discovery by American soldiers of an underground Iraqi prison where many people were living. The CNN reporter said, "Some of the men in this prison have been locked in here for over 20 years, never seeing the light of day." As soon as the American soldiers began to open the prison door, a man was heard yelling out "I afraid of light. I afraid of light." You see, the light is piercing. This man was afraid of the light.

The Light is <u>piercing</u>!

> "...He will bring to light what is hidden in darkness and will expose the motives of men's hearts" (1 Corinthians 4:5).

But, you see, people who have not lived in the light, don't understand the benefits of the light. The light enables us to see what cannot be seen in the darkness. **In the light, we gain a <u>perception</u> that we never had in the <u>dark</u>.**

> For God, who said, "Let light shine out of darkness," made his light shine in our hearts to give us the light of the knowledge of the glory of God in the face of Christ (2 Corinthians 4:6).

The Light gives <u>perception</u>!

Paul is taking us back to creation, where the world was originally in darkness, empty, and buried in the water, and then God *said*, "Let there be light". The Word of God brought light. And then, on the third day, there was a "resurrection," where the waters separated and the earth came up out of the water.

What Paul is doing is using creation as an example of salvation. You see, we were at one time in darkness (in hiding, living in secrecy), we were empty, and we were buried in sin - until God's Word brought light. It all begins with light! "For God who said 'Let Light shine...'"

<u>Heaven Came Down and Glory Filled My Soul,</u> one of our older hymns, includes this verse:
> O what a wonderful, wonderful day—
> Day I will never forget;
> After I'd wandered in darkness away,
> Jesus my Saviour I met.
> O what a tender, compassionate friend—
> He met the need of my heart;

Shadows dispelling, with joy I am telling,
He made all the darkness depart.
*John W. Peterson, 1921

But not only does the light give perception, let's notice something else that the light does. Please look with me at 1 John. 1:5-7:

> [5] This is the message we have heard from him and declare to you: God is light; in him there is no darkness at all. [6] If we claim to have fellowship with him yet walk in the darkness, we lie and do not live by the truth. [7] But if we walk in the light, as he is in the light, we have fellowship with one another, and the blood of Jesus, his Son, purifies us from all sin.

According to verse 7, what is the one requirement to being purified from all sin? The answer begins with the word "if…" "If we walk in the light…" Now we see that -

The Light is <u>purifying</u>!

We experience forgiveness of our sins when we come into the light. **The light overcomes the <u>darkness</u>, and we begin to experience freedom from secret <u>sins</u>, freedom from <u>hiding</u>, and freedom from <u>deception</u>.**

When my son, Joshua, was born, he had yellow jaundice (hyperbilirubinemia), which is a condition where the body is not capable of removing the old red blood cells and replacing them with new red blood cells. The problem is that those old red blood cells can become toxic and poisonous, and can eventually lead to death. What the nurses did was to place Joshua under the light, because the light enables the body to remove the old red blood cells and replace them with the new ones. The light is purifying!

You see, sin is like a fungus; it grows best in the dark. But, if we will drag our sin into the light, the light will sap it of strength. Like a fungus exposed to the light, it will wither and eventually die. We will discover that walking in the light is purifying!

But, not only does the light give perception, not only is the light purifying, but let us notice something else about the light as we turn to Romans 13:12-14:

> [12] The night is nearly over; the day is almost here. So let us put aside the deeds of darkness and put on the armor of light. [13] Let us behave decently, as in the daytime, not in orgies and drunkenness, not in sexual immorality and debauchery, not in dissension and jealousy. [14] Rather, clothe yourselves with the Lord Jesus Christ, and do not think about how to gratify the desires of the flesh.

The Light is <u>protective</u>!

Friend, the above verses tell us that the light is <u>armor</u>, and armor protects a soldier from the attacks of the enemy. The enemy always shoots at us in the darkness but, if we walk in the light, we have protection from his assaults. This is an important principle to understand: Light, in the spiritual realm, is armor.

The understanding of this very passage brought about many changes in my life. I remember when I first understood that the light was like armor; that it was protective. I decided to make some big changes. Since I had been viewing pornography on my computer, I had previously given it away to my pastor. But after a year, we decided I could get a new computer. I asked my wife to view the history on it every day. If there were no history, it would mean I had deleted it. Since I had been sinning by calling 900 numbers on the phone, I asked my wife to look at each phone call on the phone bill, and to call any numbers she did not recognize. And since I had been viewing pornography at hotels, I asked my wife to call the hotel after I had left to verify what charges were on the room.

I simply did not want there to be any place for the evil one to hide in my life, no dark corners, no unlit alleys, no private rooms or areas where sin could hide. But, not only does the light give perception, not only is it purifying, not only is it protective like armor, but let us notice one final thing about the light from Lamentations 2:14:

> The visions of your prophets were false and worthless; they did not expose your sin to ward off your captivity. The oracles they gave you were false and misleading.

The Light is a <u>preventative</u>: it prevents <u>captivity</u>!

In Lamentations, Jeremiah weeps over the sin, the low spiritual condition, and the captivity of the nation of Israel. God tells him that the reason the people went into captivity is because the prophets did not expose the sin of the nation, so that the nation might repent. Had the prophets exposed the sin, and the nation repented, it would have warded off their captivity. That's right. **<u>Exposing</u> the sin would have prevented their captivity!**

Let us be really clear on this: leaving sin covered, by refusing to expose it, leads to captivity. **We become captives to the <u>power</u> of sin while it is <u>hidden</u> and kept secret.** But, if we expose it, we ward off captivity and live as free men! The light is a preventative. It prevents captivity.

During my years of slavery to pornography, I appeared to be a respectable man. I was an airline captain, had been to seminary, and was outwardly "successful" with a good

47

family. But, in secret I was a different man. I would layover in hotels and had much private time. The pornographic channels in the hotel room would draw me powerfully and I would give in repeatedly, year after year after year. I would pray against it, read my Bible, and plan not to fall, but as soon as I would get to the privacy of my hotel room, lust would take over and I would plunge into pornography.

This same scenario, or one like it, is played out all across the world, as people hide in prisons of darkness, living lives of secret sin. Some hide in the dark dungeon of alcoholism; some live the secret life of pornography and sexual immorality; others hide their homosexuality, or their drug addiction, or their gambling.

What was happening to me during those years, that I had no power to overcome sin? Why did I give in time and time again, especially when I had prayed so much to not give in? The answer is that sinning was all done in the darkness, in secret, where sin thrives.

I can't tell you the relief I feel now that I am no longer sneaking around, trying to hide my sin, always looking over my shoulder to see if I would be caught. Though it was somewhat embarrassing to drag my sin out into the light, it was also freeing. The man in Iraq who was screaming "I afraid of light" did not understand that *the light meant freedom*!

Setting Captives Free course member John wrote, *"I have been hiding, not only in the sinful darkness, but also in groups that are anonymous. I had not understood before, but now I see that the light is armor, and that the light prevents captivity. I have dragged my sin into the light with my pastor and then my wife, and have cut off any and all access to it. Lord willing, I will have light shining in every area of my life now. The devil had convinced me that if I said one word about my sin, it would be all over for me. But he was lying. The truth sets you free!"*

We have seen in this session that the light brings perception, that the light is purifying, that the light is protective, and that the light is a preventative; it wards off captivity.

Ye dwellers in darkness
With sin blinded eyes,
The Light of the world is Jesus!
Go, wash, at His bidding,
And light will arise.
The Light of the world is Jesus!
* Words and Music by Philip P. Bless, 1875

The people walking in darkness have seen a great light; on those living in the land of the shadow of death a light has dawned (Isaiah 9:2).

Come, O house of Jacob, let us walk in the light of the LORD (Isaiah 2:5).

So how do we walk in the light of the Lord? What specific things can we do to ensure that we are ongoingly purified and protected by the light? Let me close this session with **three specific things we can do every day to help ensure that we are walking in the light:**

1. Read our <u>Bibles</u>. (Psalm 119:130; John 1).

2. <u>Confess</u> our sins. (James 5:16; 1 John 1:9). If there is any unconfessed sin in our lives, there is darkness dwelling there. Confess it, and let the truth set you free. Regarding confession of sin, be careful about this. Here are some instructions to follow:

- If confession needs to happen, request assistance from the body of Christ. Ask a pastor, elder, or small group leader to be with you during the confession to help ensure a godly response on all sides.
- Use biblical terms, and ask for forgiveness. Don't minimize the sin, call it what the Bible calls it, and then ask forgiveness.
- Present your plan for leaving sin behind, such as how you have radically amputated the source of the sin, that you are taking the Setting Captives Free 60-day course, to whom you are now being accountable (providing names and contact information may be helpful), and that you are checking in with the pastor or elders once a week to ensure them of your ongoing progress, etc.
- Never share details. The confession can be straightforward and honest, without minimizing whatsoever, and yet not share any of the details of the sin. The sharing of details may plant thoughts in the minds of others which make it difficult to forgive. Be firm; no sharing of details.

3. Find someone to whom you will be <u>accountable</u> (Hebrews 3:13), someone with whom you can share anything. This person could, and eventually should, be your wife, as two become one. But, initially, it may be another man who walks with you when tempted, who prays for you to overcome by God's grace, and who encourages your spiritual growth or lovingly rebukes as necessary.

Let me close with a statement found in the book of Job, which closely parallels that of my own life, and perhaps yours:

> [27] Then he comes to men and says, 'I sinned, and perverted what was right, but I did not get what I deserved. [28] He redeemed my soul from going down to the pit, and I will live to enjoy the light' (Job 33:27-28).

My secret sins were very grievous and they lasted a very long time. But God redeemed me, He saved me, He is cleansing and purifying me, and now I have discovered that the Light is not merely to be walked in or tolerated, but it is also to be thoroughly enjoyed. Yes, I will testify that it is more enjoyable to have no areas of secrecy, no secret corners of darkness, to live in the Light, and to enjoy the Light!

Men of Honor - Session Four Worksheet

Islam is the fastest-growing _____ in the world because it attracts _____.

To stem the tide of men _____ the church, it will take men finding freedom from the grip of _____, men taking seriously the admonition to _____ themselves, men truly becoming men of _____!

Because of the oneness of _____, what happens in the husband's life affects his _____.

[19] This is the verdict: Light has come into the world, but men loved darkness instead of light because their deeds were evil. [20] Everyone who does evil hates the light, and will not come into the light for fear that his deeds will be exposed (John 3:19-20)

The Light is _____!

"…He will bring to light what is hidden in darkness and will expose the motives of men's hearts" (1 Corinthians 4:5).

In the light, we gain a _____ that we never had in the _____.

For God, who said, "Let light shine out of darkness," made his light shine in our hearts to give us the light of the knowledge of the glory of God in the face of Christ (2 Corinthians 4:6).

The Light gives _____!

What Paul is doing is using _____ as an example of salvation.

[5] This is the message we have heard from him and declare to you: God is light; in him there is no darkness at all. [6] If we claim to have fellowship with him yet walk in the darkness, we lie and do not live by the truth. [7] But if we walk in the light, as he is in the light, we have fellowship with one another, and the blood of Jesus, his Son, purifies us from all sin (1 John 1:5-7).

The Light is _____!

The light overcomes the _____, and we begin to experience freedom from secret_____ _____, freedom from _____, and freedom from _____.

¹² The night is nearly over; the day is almost here. So let us put aside the deeds of darkness and put on the armor of light. ¹³ Let us behave decently, as in the daytime, not in orgies and drunkenness, not in sexual immorality and debauchery, not in dissension and jealousy. ¹⁴ Rather, clothe yourselves with the Lord Jesus Christ, and do not think about how to gratify the desires of the flesh (Romans 13:12-14).

The Light is _____!

Light, in the spiritual realm, is _____.

The visions of your prophets were false and worthless; they did not expose your sin to ward off your captivity. The oracles they gave you were false and misleading (Lamentations 2:14).

The Light is a _____**: it prevents** _____!

_____ the sin would have prevented their captivity!

We become captives to the _____ of sin while it is _____ and kept secret.

The people walking in darkness have seen a great light; on those living in the land of the shadow of death a light has dawned (Isaiah 9:2).

Come, O house of Jacob, let us walk in the light of the LORD (Isaiah 2:5).

Three specific things we can do every day to help ensure that we are walking in the light:

  1. Read our _____. (Psalm 119:130; John 1).

  2. _____ our sins. (James 5:16; 1 John 1:9).

  3. Find someone to whom we will be _____. (Hebrews 3:13).

²⁷ Then he comes to men and says, 'I sinned, and perverted what was right, but I did not get what I deserved. ²⁸ He redeemed my soul from going down to the pit, and I will live to enjoy the light' (Job 33:27-28).

Men of Honor — Session Four
Discussion Questions

(Main session - John 3:19-20, 1 Corinthians 4:5, 2 Corinthians 4:6, 1 John 1:5-7, Romans 13:12-14, Lamentations 2:14, Isaiah 9:2, Job 33:27-28; Small groups - Ephesians 5:3-13, John 8:12, Psalm 56:13, Colossians 1:13, Psalm 89:15-17, 2 Timothy 2:21-22)

Question 1. Please read Ephesians 5:3-13. As presented in this passage, what are the "deeds of darkness," and what is the "fruit of the light?" How is "darkness" related to (or associated with, related to, connected to, or linked to) "secrecy" in this passage?

Question 2. Please read John 8:12. Jesus said, "Whoever follows Me will never walk in darkness." What connection is there between following Jesus and walking in the light? Are you following Jesus, and also walking in the light?

Question 3. Please read Psalm 56:13. In this passage, David is praising God for deliverance from His enemies. He states that he had been delivered both from death, and also from stumbling. But why? According to David, for what purpose had he been delivered from death and from stumbling?

Question 4. Please read Psalm 89:15-17. According to this passage, what are the characteristics of those who have learned to praise the Lord, and who *walk in the light* of His presence? Are you walking in the light and experiencing these blessings?

Question 5. We learned from 2 Timothy 2:21-22 that a man of honor cleanses himself from all impurity. Why is it necessary to "walk in the light" in order to be cleansed from all impurity, and thereby become a man of honor? Are you committed to walking in the light, to ongoing cleansing from all impurity, and to living as a man of honor? Is there any "secrecy" (hiding of sin) that you wish to drag into the light right now?

Discussion Leader

and/or

Facilitator
Notes

Men of Honor - Session One
Discussion Leader/Facilitator Notes

Main Session - 2 Timothy 2:20-21, Acts 19:18-20, 1 John 2:14, Genesis 35:1-5, 1 Peter 1:22, Psalms 23:5, Psalms 103:5, John 7:37-39; Small Groups - Isaiah 55:1-3, Ephesians 4:19, Jeremiah 2:13.

The teaching for the first session is found in John 4, the story of Jesus and the woman at the well. The point of the passage is that the woman, while involved in multiple and ongoing relationships, was "thirsting." Jesus invited her to drink from Him and, by so doing, promised she would "never thirst" again. In other words, she would be satisfied in Christ and would not need to pursue one relationship after another, because her cravings and longings would be fulfilled in Jesus.

We want to apply this same truth to the men of our church, and help them to quench their spiritual thirst in Jesus. "Thirst" shows up in men turning to other "water sources" such as pornography, illicit relationships, alcohol and/or drugs, overeating, gambling, or other sinful habits. Jesus' words, "He who drinks this water will thirst again" applies to these other "water sources," as they leave the soul parched and dehydrated. Like salt water, pornography (and all other forms of impurity) only creates more thirst, drying up the soul.

When Jesus said the woman would "thirst again" when drinking of "this water," it is clear that Jesus was not merely speaking of the physical water in the well (for it is quite obvious that we will "thirst again" when drinking physical water), but rather He was using the water in the well as an analogy of the "waters" of sin (in the woman's case, multiple relationships), and how they do not meet the deep needs of the heart; they do not "quench the thirst" of the human soul.

The point of the passage is that, if the woman would turn to Jesus and begin to "drink" from Him, her "thirst" would be quenched. And this is the same way that men and women find freedom from the perpetual "thirst" cycle of "addiction." When our souls are satisfied in Jesus Christ, we are no longer "thirsty."

The passage we will study for the small group teaching/interaction session is Isaiah 55. This passage is an invitation to the "thirsty" to come to God (and His Word) and find in Him "water which will satisfy." It asks the question, "Why spend your labor on what does not satisfy?" Therefore, the contrast is between God (and His Word) which is true water to the soul, and "that which does not satisfy."

Isaiah 55 can be used in your teaching/discussion session to both reinforce the principle Jesus taught in John 4 (that of finding freedom from spiritual "thirst" by quenching our souls in Christ), and also as an invitation for men to switch "water sources" from "that which does not satisfy" to God and His Word.

Before class, please review Jeremiah 2:13 to see how it relates to today's subject.

The discussion questions are below. Please review them in advance in order to be familiar with the material. Our purpose is to reach the hearts of the men, not to merely impart knowledge. Information is not the same as transformation, and it is our desire to impact the hearts and lives of the men, resulting in a true transformation.

> [1] "Come, all you who are thirsty, come to the waters; and you who have no money, come, buy and eat! Come, buy wine and milk without money and without cost. [2] Why spend money on what is not bread, and your labor on what does not satisfy? Listen, listen to me, and eat what is good, and your soul will delight in the richest of fare. [3] Give ear and come to me; hear me, that your soul may live. I will make an everlasting covenant with you, my faithful love promised to David.
>
> Isaiah 55:1-3

Question 1. According to Isaiah 55:1-3, who is issued the invitation? Is this "thirsty" condition physical or spiritual?

Note: The invitation in Isaiah 55:1-3 is for the "thirsty." It is to the "soul hungry" and the "soul thirsty" that the invitation is addressed, as indicated by the promised result of eating the "food" and drinking the "water" offered: "your *soul* will delight…"

Right here you might ask your group of men to list some of the "symptoms" of spiritual "thirst." That is, what is life like for a man who is spiritually "thirsty?"

Question 2. The invitation in Isaiah 55:1-3 is for those who "thirst" to "come to the waters." But where are the "waters?" How does verse 3 help us to understand the answer?

Note: God makes the invitation to come to Him and drink, and then tells them *how* to do so in verse 3: "Give *ear* and *listen* to me; *hear* me…" So the "water" is in the Word of God. As we "listen" and "hear God" for the purpose of obeying Him, we begin to "drink" of the Living Water.

Question 3. If we "drink" by "listening to God" in His Word, what are the results of drinking in the Word, according to verse 2?

Note: Verse 2 tells us that if we listen to God in His Word, our souls will *delight*. Receiving God's Word produces a *rejoicing* in the heart and *elation* in the soul.

Question 4. What are the results of drinking in the Word, according to verse 3?

Notes: Verse 3 tells us that the result of drinking the Word of God is life to the soul. Life! When we listen to God in His Word, our hearts begin to rejoice in Him.

At this point, you might want to contrast the life of the "thirsting" man with the life of the "rejoicing" man. In question 1, you asked the men to state some of the symptoms of "thirsting," and here you have an opportunity to ask them to state some of the results of those who learn to quench their thirst and satisfy their appetites in Jesus Christ.

Question 5. How does this verse go with today's teaching? "Having lost all sensitivity, they have given themselves over to sensuality so as to indulge in every kind of impurity, *with a continual lust for more*" Ephesians 4:19 (emphasis added).

Note: Ephesians 4:19 describes those who give themselves over to impurity; they "continually lust for more." This truth is identical to Jesus' words, "he who drinks this water will *thirst again.*" The point to make is that the lifestyle of impurity produces unsatisfied cravings and unfulfilled longings within the heart, which require us to go farther in sin, and go deeper in sin, to attempt to find satisfaction.

Help your group of men understand that this lifestyle is in direct contrast to Jesus' words in John 4, "he who drinks the water I give him will *never thirst*" (emphasis added).

Question 6. What are your thoughts about this quote from Charles Spurgeon? "Men are in a restless pursuit after satisfaction in earthly things. They will exhaust themselves in the deceitful delights of sin, and, finding them to be vanity, and emptiness, they will become very perplexed and disappointed. But they will continue their fruitless search. Though wearied, they still stagger forward under the influence of spiritual madness, and though there is no result to be reached except that of everlasting disappointment, yet they press forward. They have no forethought for their eternal state; the present hour absorbs them. They turn to another and another of earth's broken cisterns, hoping to find water where not a drop was ever discovered yet."

Note: Charles Spurgeon compared the life of impurity to "spiritual madness" resulting in a "fruitless search" for water, where no water has ever been found.

You might want to read Jeremiah 2:13 to your group, noting that when we turn from God to satisfy our flesh, we turn from a Living Spring to "broken cisterns."

> "My people have committed two sins: They have forsaken me, the spring
> of living water, and have dug their own cisterns, broken cisterns that
> cannot hold water.
>
> Jeremiah 2:13

Note: This would be a good opportunity to ask your group of men from what "broken cisterns" the world drinks today. We want them to name pornography and sexual impurity, alcohol, drugs and cigarettes, gambling, etc. But they could also be prompted to name "good" things such as "climbing the corporate ladder," workaholism, materialism, or any of the more seemingly innocent activities which might keep men from drinking in the water of the Word of God.

Question 7. Verse 2 of Isaiah 55 above asks an important question: "Why spend money on what does not satisfy? Have you spent money (or time) on that which does not satisfy?

Note: Here is an opportunity to help the men to open up and share. It would be helpful for you to lead in this by sharing any areas in which you have spent time or money on "that which does not satisfy." If others share after you, then the Holy Spirit might prompt you and others to pray for those who have confessed to involvement in any impurity, encouraging them to now turn from "that which does not satisfy" to the Living Water in the Word of God.

Your Comments:

Men of Honor — Session Two
Discussion Leader/Facilitator Notes

Main Session - Matthew 15:18-20, Isaiah 53:4-8; Matthew 5:29-30, John 6:50-57; Luke 11:24-27, Ecclesiastes 4:9-12, 2 Timothy 2:21-22; Small Groups - James 1:19-21; 1 Corinthians 5:6-8

The teaching in session two is on the foundations for freedom from impurity. The three concepts taught were *radical amputation*, *radical appropriation*, and *radical accountability*. Like a three-legged stool, each truth is important in helping one who is in bondage to habitual sin to find freedom in Jesus Christ.

The first truth listed is radical amputation. The implementation of this biblical concept in the life of one seeking to escape sin's power is essential. The world would teach us to "wean ourselves off" that which has taken us captive, but this method is futile for finding long-term freedom. The Bible clearly teaches that, in order to be free from sin, there must be a complete separation from it, and a radical stance against it.

As small group leaders, you will most likely deal with the specific questions of how one might "radically amputate" his source of stumbling. Scenarios abound with regard to how to eliminate access, and we should be willing to help each person who asks. Often this requires creative thinking, as in the case of the man who is a computer programmer and is enslaved to Internet pornography. There is always a solution. For instance, for the computer programmer, it may be possible to ask his boss to move the computer to a public area. If he works at home, he could open up his work room and make it viewable to his family and install the Safe Eyes filter. As a last resort, he might consider changing jobs. There are ways to overcome any objection to radical amputation; it is just that sometimes we must help the person think creatively. One thing I do is to remind the person that while involved in habitual sin, we were creative in how to hide the sin, how to avoid getting caught, how to schedule our time so as to be able to indulge our flesh. Now, in turning from sin, we should be just as creative in finding ways to cut it off.

Radical appropriation of Christ is just as important as radical amputation. If we can help the men to begin feasting on Jesus Christ, through the Word of God, church, worship, witnessing, etc., they will have secured their freedom in Christ. If radical amputation is "slamming the door" to sin, then radical appropriation is "bolting the lock," to make returning to sin extremely unappealing. As small group leaders, we mainly teach this truth through example. We can share how we feed on God's Word often, how we read for the purpose of obeying, how we enjoy sermon tapes, how we love church, worship, etc. In other words, there is no void in our lives that would pull us back into sin, for we are full in Christ. Our cup overflows with His Living Water and, therefore, we are not seeking something to fill the emptiness.

Finally, radical accountability is important for the first few months/year for the one desiring freedom. Remember, accountability is not "supporting" someone who continually falls to sin; rather, it is utilizing encouragement, exhortation, and rebuke when needed.

Question 1. In light of Matthew 5:29-30, why is it important to be radical in fighting against sin? Why does the "weaning from sin" principle, as taught by the world, not work?

Note: In Matthew 5:29-30 Jesus instructed us to "do whatever it takes" to be free from impurity. The reason it is important to be radical in removing access to that which would cause us to stumble is because sin is radical in its attempts to destroy us. Oftentimes a person will raise a scenario of how it is seemingly impossible for him to radically amputate all access. But if we give in and agree with him that it is impossible, we have not helped him to freedom. However, if we hold firm and do not budge on this principle, it is possible he will begin thinking of creative ways to obey Jesus and eliminate access to that which causes him to stumble. As the discussion leader, it is important that we help men to understand that this principle is non-negotiable, and that their freedom from habitual sin depends upon their implementing it in their lives.

Question 2. Which two of the three principles of freedom are found in James 1:19-22? Why is the implementation of both of these truths important to our freedom?

Note: James 1:19-21 tells us to "get rid of all moral filth" which speaks of "amputation" and then to "humbly accept the Word" which is comparable to "appropriation." It would be helpful to remind the men that the Scripture commands the riddance of "all" moral filth. Again, this can be perceived as somewhat radical, but it is essential to finding freedom. The "radical appropriation" is found in the instruction to not merely "hear" the Word, but rather "do what it says." "Read and do, read and do"; this is radical appropriation.

Question 3. Please read 1 Corinthians 5:6-8. How does this passage teach two out of three foundational truths to freedom from habitual sin?

Note: This passage is a reminder of the Passover, recorded in Exodus 12, where the Israelites were redeemed from slavery in Egypt. The Israelites were to kill the Passover lamb, apply its blood to their doorposts, and by so doing, would be saved from death and released from bondage. On the day of the death of the lamb, the Israelites were instructed to remove all yeast (leaven) from their bread and from their homes. Tradition tells us that they would light candles and make a careful search throughout their homes, looking in every corner and in every obscure place, to ensure that all leaven was removed. They were then to celebrate the feast of unleavened bread, enjoying both the meat of the Passover lamb and the unleavened bread, in *celebration* of their freedom from slavery.

1 Corinthians 5:6-8 tells us to "get rid of the old yeast," the yeast of "malice and wickedness of all kinds" and is kin to the idea of radical amputation. Then the passage

tells us to "keep the festival," indicating that the Christian life should be one of continual celebration of freedom from bondage to sin, through the death of Jesus Christ. Celebrating the Feast is kin to radical appropriation where we feast on Jesus as both our Passover Lamb and as our Bread of Life.

Question 4. According to 1 Corinthians 5:7, what motivation does Paul provide for removing all sin and wickedness from our lives? Why is this compelling and urgent?

Note: Paul's stated motivation for the command to "get rid of the old yeast" is that "Christ, our Passover Lamb, has been sacrificed." The death of Jesus Christ is in view here and, as the discussion leader, you can focus the attention of the class on the cross. It may be helpful, time permitting, to read through portions of Exodus 12 with the men, noting how the death of the lamb both released the Israelites from slavery and also was to be eaten and enjoyed, providing nourishment to those who were redeemed. The point is that the passage speaks of radical amputation (the removal of all sin), and radical appropriation (the feasting on Christ as our Passover Lamb).

Question 5. Please read 2 Timothy 2:20-21. According to this passage, upon what is being a "man of honor" dependent? What four blessings are listed to those who will cleanse themselves?

Note: As the discussion leader, help the men to see that being a man of honor is dependent upon cleansing ourselves from impurity. Focus on the blessings that come to men who will take cleansing seriously. He will be 1—an instrument for noble purposes, 2—made holy, 3—useful to the Master, and 4—prepared to do any good work.

Question 6. Please read through Ecclesiastes 4:9-12. Please discuss the importance of accountability, and of having a brother with whom to walk. What are the dangers listed in being "alone?"

Note: As the discussion leader, be willing to provide your contact information to the group and see if there are other mature men who would like to make themselves available for accountability for others.

Question 7. Application time: Have you radically amputated all access to that which has caused you to stumble? Are you "getting rid of all moral filth?" Are you "removing all the old yeast"?

Men of Honor — Session Three
Discussion Leader/Facilitator Notes

Main Session - 2 Timothy 2:22-26, Acts 11:18, 2 Corinthians 7:8-13, Psalms 51:16-17, James 4:8-10, Romans 6:20-22, Acts 26:18; Small Groups - Acts 26:15-18, 2 Timothy 2:24-26, Matthew 3:8.

Question 1. Please examine Acts 26:15-18. In this passage of Scripture, how is repentance defined?

Note: Repentance is defined as turning away from darkness and turning to the light. Further, it is defined as turning away from the power of Satan and turning to God. It is important to help the group understand that "darkness" and "the power of Satan" are related. Those practicing secret sin do so under the power of the devil. The way to be free from it is to turn to the Light, that is, to Jesus Christ and to truthful, transparent living. In turning from darkness to light, we are turning from the power of Satan to God.

Question 2. According to Acts 26:15-18, what are the conditions of one who has not yet repented?

Note: Those who have not repented are characterized by the following conditions:

- They are blind, and in need of having their eyes opened. Obviously, this is not a reference to physical blindness, but rather to a person's inability to see the truth about sin and their need for the Savior.
- They are in darkness, and in need of turning to the Light. Darkness in Scripture refers to ignorance, unbelief, deceit, secret sins, and sinful bondage, etc.
- They are under the power of Satan, and in need of turning to God. Satan holds men and women captive through lies and deceit and through the practice of habitual, secret sins.
- They are unforgiven, and in need of repentance so that they might experience forgiveness.

Question 3. In this same passage, what are the stated benefits of repentance?

Note: The stated benefits of repentance are:

- ". . .that they might receive forgiveness of sins." The blessing of forgiveness comes to those who repent, who turn away from darkness and the power of Satan, and turn to the Light and the power of God. Small group leaders should help the class see that in Scripture "forgiveness" is related to and follows "repentance."
- ". . a place among those who are sanctified by faith in Me." This is a clear reference to salvation, and teaches us that eternal life is conditional upon repentance from sin. There is no "place" in heaven for the unrepentant. Rather, repentance secures the place for the repentant, and gives evidence that he or she belongs to Christ.

Question 4. Please examine 2 Timothy 2:24-26. What are the conditions of one who has not repented?

Note: According to 2 Timothy 2:24-26, one who has not repented is:

- "opposed" to God's servant
- ignorant of the knowledge of truth
- out of their right mind, and in need of "coming to their senses"
- trapped by the devil, and captive to his will

Question 5. According to 2 Timothy 2:24-26, how, specifically, was Timothy to treat and interact with those who were trapped in sin?

Note: Timothy was instructed to not argue with those who are argumentative, nor to enter into "stupid arguments and quarrels." (Verse 25) Instead, he was to gently instruct those who want to argue, he was to be patient with them, and was to trust God to grant them repentance.

There is a simple acronym to help us remember this method of dealing with those who are trapped in sin and who wish to argue against the truth, and against their own freedom. It is the GAP method.

> **G**entle
> **A**ble to teach
> **P**atient

Question 6. According to 2 Timothy 2:24-26, what are the stated benefits of repentance?

The stated benefits of repentance are that we:

- are led to a knowledge of the truth
- come to our senses
- escape the trap of the devil

Question 7. What does Matthew 3:8 tell us about genuine repentance?

Note: Matthew 3:8 tells us that "fruit" accompanies repentance. That is, there are results that become evidenced over time that indicate repentance. This is difficult to measure, at times, because fruit takes time to grow.

The way it would look in the life of one involved, for example, in pornography, is that the person is finished with the false intimacy that pornography portrays, and instead he is now able to enjoy real fellowship and genuine intimacy with his wife. He begins to lose his critical spirit, his anger toward and high expectancy of others, his self-righteous and

64

haughty attitude, and instead begins to operate in grace and kindness, and in love and humility and understanding of others.

Your Comments:

Men of Honor — Session Four
Discussion Leader/Facilitator Notes

Main session - John 3:19-20, 1 Corinthians 4:5, 2 Corinthians 4:6, 1 John 1:5-7, Romans 13:12-14, Lamentations 2:14, Isaiah 9:2, Job 33:27-28; Small groups - Ephesians 5:3-13, John 8:12, Psalm 56:13, Colossians 1:13, Psalm 89:15-17, 2 Timothy 2:21-22

Question 1. Please read Ephesians 5:3-13. As presented in this passage, what are the "deeds of darkness," and what is the "fruit of the light?" How is "darkness" correlated with "secrecy" in this passage?

Note: The "deeds of darkness" are listed as sexual immorality, impurity, greed, foolish talk, coarse joking, etc. (verses 4-5); whereas the "fruit of the light" is "all goodness, righteousness and truth" (verse 9). Verses 11 and 12 correlate "darkness" with "secrecy" by using the word "for" in verse 12. We are to "have nothing to do with the *deeds of darkness*"...*for* it is shameful to even mention what the disobedient do *in secret*."

In your discussion group, it will be helpful to explain that the power of sin resides in darkness, and the way to be free of secret sin (or deeds done in darkness) is to "expose them" (verse 11). Sin that is exposed to the light is weakened. It is always somewhat embarrassing to expose secret sin, but those who wish to be free of the power of darkness will do so.

Question 2. Please read John 8:12. Jesus said, "Whoever follows Me will never walk in darkness." What connection is there between following Jesus and walking in the light? Are you following Jesus, <u>and also</u> walking in the light?

Note: The connection needs to be made that following Jesus Christ is what enables us to be free of a life of darkness. In other words, it is not merely the exposing of secret sin that needs to happen, but also the complete and unreserved commitment to follow Christ. It is not merely the stopping of secret sin that is needed but, since Jesus is the Light of the world, there must be a following after Christ, a pursuing Christ, a joyful walking with Him daily. This fellowship with Christ, which results in joyful following of Him, is that which keeps us from walking in darkness.

You may want to remind your discussion group of Peter's fall here, when He denied Jesus three times (Matthew 26:69-75); this was a time when Peter "walked in darkness". Yet his fall didn't happen suddenly; rather we can trace the fall back to when He began distancing himself from Jesus (see Matthew 26: 58).

The summary of the matter is that walking in darkness (living in secret sin) is avoided when we follow close to Jesus, the "Light of the world".

65

Question 3. Please read Psalm 56:13. In this passage, David is praising God for deliverance from His enemies. He states that he had been delivered both from death, and also from stumbling. But why? According to David, for what purpose had he been delivered from death and from stumbling?

Note: David said that God delivered him from death and his feet from stumbling, "so that he might walk before God in the light of life." This is precisely the same way that God deals with His children today. Jesus' death on the cross delivers us from death, and the work of the Holy Spirit in our hearts helps us to walk uprightly. The purpose of this work of God is so that we would walk before God in the light. He did not die for us and work in our hearts so that we might return to secret sin, but so that we might live with integrity, walk transparently, and avoid the power of sin, which is darkness.

Consider Colossians 1:13:

> For he has rescued us from the dominion of darkness and brought us into the kingdom of the Son he loves (Colossians 1:13).

Note: God rescued and delivered David from death and stumbling (the dominion of darkness) and brought him into the kingdom of Jesus Christ (walking in the Light of Life). He does the same for all His children. (See 1 Peter 2:9).

Question 4. Please read Psalm 89:15-17. According to this passage, what are the characteristics of those who have learned to praise the Lord, and who *walk in the light* of His presence? Are you walking in the light and experiencing these blessings?

Note: Those who have learned to walk in the light are:

- Rejoicing in God's Name all day long. They have cause for rejoicing, for since exposing their sin to the light, it no longer has power over them. They experience freedom from secret sin, so they are given cause for rejoicing all day long.
- Exult in the righteousness of Christ. They are covered in the light of Christ's righteousness and, as such, there is genuine worship in their hearts. They are no longer hiding, but are surrounded by and enveloped in the righteousness of Christ. The light has become their armor, and therefore they exult in the righteousness of Christ which surrounds them.
- Glory in Christ's strength. They have known of the power of darkness, now they know of the power of God to deliver them from it.

All three of these benefits speak of worship (rejoicing, exulting in, and glorying in). Help your discussion group understand that when a man becomes free from hiding and secret sin, he becomes a worshiper in spirit and in truth. He becomes a **Man of Honor**, and a man of honor is one who is cleansed from past sin and is worshiping God.

Question 5. We learned from 2 Timothy 2:21-22 that a man of honor cleanses himself from all impurity. Why is it necessary to "walk in the light" in order to be cleansed from all impurity, and thereby become a **Man of Honor**? Are you committed to walking in the light, to ongoing cleansing from all impurity, and to living as a man of honor? Is there any "secrecy" (hiding of sin) that you wish to drag into the light right now?

Note: this question is for discussion.

Your Comments:

MEN OF HONOR

Response Form

Please indicate your evaluation by number:
5. Extremely helpful 4.Very helpful 3. Interesting
2. Little relevance 1. No relevance at all

_____Addressing the topic of sexual purity issues

_____Presentations were biblical and helpful to me

_____Men at my table related well

_____Discussion questions were engaging

Please check if applicable– you will be contacted in strict confidentiality

_____I am struggling with pornography.

_____I am struggling with another life-dominating sin, that of _____

_____I am willing to complete a 60-day online Bible study course from Setting Captives

Free, and to be in weekly contact (for the 60 days) with an accountability partner.

First Name: _____

Phone or e-mail: _____